OFF THE CUFF & OVER THE COLLAR:

COMMON SENSE CATHOLICISM

Bishop John McCarthy

With
Jill Grimes, MD,
and Tom Borders

Greenhills Publishing
Austin, Texas

ISBN-13: 978-0989262408
ISBN-10: 0989262405

*This book is dedicated to our newly appointed
Pope Francis, the 266th successor to St. Peter*

TABLE OF CONTENTS

FOREWORD

Heads turn and smiles ignite across the congregation with the recognition that the priest heading towards the altar to celebrate mass is our Bishop Emeritus, John McCarthy. We happily anticipate a mass and sermon that will help us to better understand both traditional scripture readings and today's practical application of God's Word. *And it certainly doesn't hurt that we are guaranteed some laughter along the way*. Although there are many vibrant Catholic communities, zest and joy are sadly often missing from Catholic masses today. With due respect and appreciation to every man who has chosen to dedicate his life to the priesthood, we recognize that Bishop McCarthy has been especially blessed with Irish wit and wisdom that help draw us into our Eucharistic celebration, rejuvenating our faith in a very special way.

Over the years, many of us wondered how we could bottle up and distribute Bishop McCarthy's insights beyond our church walls. Tom Borders initially chose to pursue an audiovisual medium, culminating in numerous hours of videotaped interviews with the Bishop both reflecting on his past and addressing current Catholic controversies. Jill Grimes favors the written word, and so emerged her *Thursdays with Bishop,* much like *Tuesdays with Morrie*. Bishop McCarthy and Jill began meeting for a couple hours each Thursday afternoon, delving into all things Catholic. Then in April of 2010, the Bishop's blog "Common Sense Catholicism" premiered, answering the Vatican's call for an Internet presence, and thus propelling Bishop McCarthy's daily reflections into cyberspace. Within these three forums, the full spectrum of Catholicism is addressed, from our Sacraments and Canon Law to our rituals, liturgical seasons, Heaven and Hell, marriage and divorce, birth and death, priests and nuns, and lighter topics such as favorite hymns, humor and even chocolate advent calendars. The sub-jects also expand into worldly applications of Jesus's directives, such as the Bishop's pet peeves regarding bullying, teasing, gossip, fears, church poli-tics and mental illness. (Check out the "McCarthy Rule" under teasing for some common sense Christianity!)

Somewhat unexpectedly, the Bishop found himself wading into deep-er waters…including such topics as papal infallibility, married or women priests, abortion, end of life issues and homosexuality. What started out to be a collection of sermons and lighthearted Christian advice evolved into a more intense examination of our Catholic traditions, structure, and indeed, our core beliefs. Ultimately, this book represents a collaboration of the Bishop's musings across time, places and media into one package. Bishop McCarthy is first and foremost a devoted Catholic priest, driven by an intense desire to extend the message of his beloved Jesus of Nazareth to all who will hear. He has utilized every form of media throughout his extended career- from newspaper, magazines and virtually every type of printed material, to radio, television and Internet. Although the media format has changed, Bishop McCarthy's healing message from our Lord has remained the same. We pray that you will smile, laugh and be touched by the Holy Spirit as you hear Bishop McCarthy speak to you – "*off the cuff, and over the collar,*" with his Common Sense Catholicism. Last but not least, we invite you to join us in praying for our new leader, Pope Francis, as he helps shape the future of our magnificent Church. *Amen!*

—*Jill Grimes and Tom Borders*

INTRODUCTION

Welcome into a book that I hope you will find a happy mixture of humor and seriousness, law, and laughter. I wrote this book for two interlocking reasons. The first reason is that I love the Church with all my heart. I chose to give myself to the Church when I was ordained a priest at age twenty-six. That love is still pervasive in my life. The second reason, however, is that for roughly the last fifteen years, I have experienced great sadness and disappointment regarding developments in the Church. Problems, misunderstandings, and scandals abound.

My objective in writing this book is to place my dreams for a more effective Catholic Church before large numbers of people, and I hope that those dreams might be a source of encouragement to them. I am not the only one who has experienced disappointment and sadness over developments within Catholicism, and it may be that others might see themselves sharing in my dreams, and that somehow those dreams could lead to and strengthen the virtue of hope. Additionally, I am excited and optimistic about the early actions of our newly appointed Pope Francis, and pray for his success in guiding us onward through the fog.

I believe in Jesus Christ. I believe He is the Son of God who came among us to draw us to Himself, and through Him to the Father. Countless millions of others share these same beliefs. So, faith is not the issue. We believe in Christ. We believe in the community of faith that He established. We believe that the Holy Spirit dwells within that community, but not necessarily that He micro-manages it on a daily basis.

Many of our concerns can be reduced to the simple world of leadership and management. The Church is in the world. It is affected by that world, sometimes adversely, and the Church is subject to the same kind of pain and harm that comes from bad administrative decisions, antiquated policies, and mistakes made when leaders cut themselves off from the faithful.

So why am I writing this book? Because I am hopeful that my views and experience, when joined with countless others who share these views and values, may generate enough interest to bring about necessary structural reforms and policies.

I love the Church. When I say that, I do not mean that it is merely an emotional attachment or a result of strong cultural ties. Those factors are certainly present in my life, but mainly I love the Church because it is simply a wonderfully beautiful gathering of human beings which not only unites us regarding the meaning and purpose of life, but motivates us to give generously of ourselves and to society in order that this valley of tears (as the Church so aptly describes the world) can be made less tearful. The encouraging light that comes from faith and hope in connection with the Church will lead all of us into our infinite goal: charity, love of God, and love of all things of God.

But is this the Church we read about on the front page of the *New York Times*?

Sadly, no it is not. However, this is my Church, the Church I love, and the Church that I am trying to serve with this book.

If you can get your mind off the tragic scandals that have beset the Church as of late, and endeavor to view it in its totality, then the beauty, mystery, love, and generosity that should mark the Church in its day-to-day life come more clearly into focus.

I don't think I have to write about the previous two thousand years. They alone are remarkable—awesome. We do have to acknowledge that for twenty centuries, this divinely willed community of faith, densely populated with human beings, struggled against every conceivable type of problem and internal weakness and never-ending destructive opposition. So, let's move on to the Church today.

Today I'm writing the book for people who have always found the Church to be somewhat confusing and mystifying. I'm actually hoping for a wide audience, one that would include not only solidly committed members of the Church, but also the indifferent Catholics as well as the hurt or even hostile, departed Catholics (regrettably counted in the millions), and finally those simply interested about this enormous old boat bouncing around in the ocean of life. And that covers almost everyone!

Originally, I was writing about very simple subjects that were a source of curiosity to many members of the Church. What is the purpose of Advent? Where do Cardinals come from? Do priests only work on Sundays? And so we progressed...

Although though some of these vignettes are about simple issues, many are serious and important. For example, I consider the abuse of teasing one of the most destructive realities in our society. I do not accept that it is natural to inflict pain on those around us to get a laugh. Someday I may write a book just on teasing!

Of course, I also touch on infinitely important subjects as death, dying, and our eternal destiny. So the book is quite a collage of all things Catholic. However, I gradually began to respond to a deeper feeling within myself that I should come to grips directly with what I consider major administrative and policy flaws.

First and foremost, I'd like to reach out to people who are perplexed and embarrassed. *I truly hope the readership will reach out to inactive Catholics who frankly don't care about their old Church.* In addition, I would hope that the book might capitalize on the innate curiosity in the American public about the inner workings of the Catholic Church. Love it or hate it, we do make news.

While I've approached this book with great seriousness, I've also really enjoyed putting it together—holding up my views against today's reality. I hope that you might enjoy my wandering thoughts as I covered this very old, yet always new and fascinating institution that endeavors to blend the human and the divine. Perhaps most importantly, *I'd like to throw open those magnificent doors to the heart of the Catholic Church, and invite you in with love and joy.*

Family and Community

"I believe absolutely that the Church is infallible. Not that it doesn't make endless mistakes, but this community of faith will never cease to teach the core message of Jesus Christ, which is necessary for the human family and ultimately for salvation. The Church will always teach that."

—Bishop John McCarthy

LIVING WITH FEAR

"Be not afraid. I go before you always!"

—*Joshua 1:9*

Long before the devastation of 9/11, I was on a hijacked plane. In the late 1960s and early 1970s, commercial airline hijackings were alarmingly frequent, with numerous flights commandeered and diverted to Cuba as either a political statement or a means of circumventing the travel ban to Cuba. I happened to be on a Delta flight from Washington, DC to Houston. The stewardess passed through the aisle, taking up the trays, and meanwhile telling everyone to remain calm, but that it appeared we were on our way to Cuba. She stopped at my row, noticing I was dressed as a priest with my Roman collar, and she whispered quietly to me, "Father, it's a little worse than I've been telling everyone. The man actually forced his way into the cabin and says he's dying, and he plans to take all of us with him! The men up in the first-class section are threatening to rush the cabin, and so I'd really appreciate if you'd come up and explain to them that that would not be a good thing to do."

Well, I'm a natural hero. I knew I was a natural hero because my legs were made out of rock-solid…Jell-O. I was scared to death! At any second, I thought the plane would plummet to the ground. Somehow, I got up into the first-class section. The flight attendant was absolutely correct. The men were all standing, filled with liquid courage and threatening to rush into the flight deck.

I've always felt that humor was a very valuable tool. I advanced up to the door, and turned around to face the men and address the group.

I reminded the men that this was a very serious situation. "As a man of God, I feel strongly moved to do something religious." They got very quiet, preparing for my prayers. I dramatically continued, "If you'd please all sit down, I'd like to …take up a collection." They all thought they were dying, but despite that, everyone started laughing. That was a very good thing! Still, there were many queries from the men, and I tried to balance my responses to them between prayerful, calming words and situational humor. For example, at one point someone asked, well, what do you want to do? "I don't know," I replied. "My God, I'm Irish, and the bar is closed!"

The brave pilot flew that plane for an hour and fifteen minutes with a gun to the back of his head, with the man behind him threatening to kill that pilot every step of the way. Finally, another member of the crew talked the hijacker into setting the plane down so we could let the women and children off. Once we were on the ground, the hijacker actually collapsed, and the pilots grabbed the gun, and then the police took him away.

Since then, I have often thought about the reality of the emotion of fear. Fear is a force deeply embedded in the human psyche. We frequently hear people being described as "fearless," but I do not think anyone is fearless. I believe that some men and women have extraordinary control over the emotion of fear so that they can keep functioning and achieving things despite the experience of fear.

Because fear is so prevalent in the human psyche, I think it must come from nature, and ultimately from God. It has great advantages. Fear can help us survive. If you're really afraid, you can fight more effectively, run faster, duck quicker, and do all the physical things required to avoid real and present danger. I think fear gives us additional motivation to adapt quickly in the face of what we perceive as danger.

However, having said that, those advantages can become disadvantages, because fear not only pumps adrenaline through the body, but can also cloud our minds so that we don't see with the same degree of clarity with which we would see if we were not afraid. Therefore, I think the rational thing to do is to admit that fear is simply a component of our makeup.

Be prepared to utilize fear when it is really an advantage (to get out of a burning house). At the same time, recognize that this emotion can be disproportionate and out of balance, and can negatively affect our thinking process and be destructive in other situations. It seems to me that we need to evaluate in our own lives how we are affected by fear, how we respond to it, and how we could maintain the necessary balance to move forward effectively in spite of it.

What to do about it? I think one of the best ways of dealing with fear is to calmly and profoundly sensitize ourselves to a deep understanding that all of our problems *are passing problems*. No matter what the situation in front of us might be, it's not permanent. Is your son in jail? Does your mother have cancer? Is your husband about to be laid off? These are real problems that bring great pain, but they are *passing*. Ultimately we are destined for an eternal life with God that is simply unending joy and happiness. If we can keep that concept in front of us at all times, we won't be so bothered by the things that frighten us. We will get upset, but we can revert to the reality that all of this is transient. This current challenge may take four months or six years, but it will indeed end.

I think that concept—that no earthly problem is permanent—is key to overcoming fear. It's easy to say, but especially if you are sixteen years old and a problem is going to last two years—well, that's an eternity! Older people, however, ought to be able to stabilize their emotional life in terms of fear with the solid understanding that this is a transient world, and what is absolutely certain, absolutely true, and absolutely going to happen is that we will share life with our God for all eternity. *Be not afraid!*

BREAKING UP IS HARD TO DO

"And I will give unto you the keys of the kingdom of heaven: and whatsoever you shall bind on earth shall be what has been bound in heaven: and whatsoever you shall loose on earth shall be what has been loosed in heaven."
—*Matthew 16:19*

Divorce is one of the greatest modern tragedies facing life in the West. Throughout much of history, marriage has been the most important social structure in a given society. That was true among the Egyptians, it was true with the Greeks and the Romans and medieval Europe, and it's still true today. As important as marriage is, because those getting married are human, there have always been a sizable number of marital unions that have been unhappy, unsuccessful, and many times destructive.

In Jewish life at the time of Christ there was divorce, and both the Greeks and the Romans gave to both parties of the marriage a means of ending a union. In the middle ages, the Church, committed as it was and is to the importance of stable family life, worked strenuously to make divorce a rarity, and in some countries, virtually impossible.

Beginning about 1800, in Europe and the West, divorce began to be more frequent, and today sadly, it is very, very common. It's hard to come up with accurate statistics, and when you see them quoted, they distinguish between rural and urban families (with the incidence of divorce in urban families being much higher).

I feel very confident in saying that the issue of divorce is the biggest source of pain and defection present in the Catholic Church in the United States today. Statistics document that roughly one half of the marriages witnessed in the United States are ending in divorce. I know of no reason why those statistics would not be almost as high for Roman Catholics, since we consistently track the larger community on such averages. While I obviously don't know the exact numbers, I would estimate that this means that when a priest is standing in the pulpit on Sunday morning, it's likely that at least one third of the people in front of him are forbidden by the Church to receive the Eucharist (*because they are or have been divorced.*) The wonderful thing is that so many of them are still committed to Sunday Mass. Of course, sadly, millions of others are not.

About ten years ago, three prominent German Bishops signed a petition to Pope John Paul II, asking him to please confront this issue. Two of those three later became Cardinals, but the Pope rebuked all of them for this suggestion. Today, some Catholic theologians are urging the Church to study the situation in the world of Greek Orthodoxy, which centuries ago developed the policy of allowing divorced Orthodox faithful to continue to receive the Eucharist following divorce and remarriage. I believe such a teaching would be a tremendous gift in our Latin Church. In fact, I urged this change in an interview given on the occasion of my retirement in 2001. Maybe that's why I was not made a Cardinal!

But seriously, let's look at this situation. *Millions of Catholics find themselves in impossible situations that cannot be altered.* They are divorced. They believe in Jesus. They believe in His presence in the Eucharist, but we tell them they are not worthy to utilize the most important gift He gave to His followers. *In my opinion, the Eucharist is a wonderful help towards being better… not a reward for being good.*

In the early Church, canonists and theologians struggled to find ways to release its members from an earlier failed marriage. That is the source of two canonical answers called the Pauline and Petrine privileges. Although it's too complicated to fully delve into here, these causes for marriage dissolution are rarely used today. (*For the curious: in short, these privileges allow for people from failed non-Christian marriages to fully enter into the Catholic Church. In other words, if a married couple consisting of a Jewish man and a Muslim woman got divorced, and subsequently one of them chose to become Catholic, he or she could become a fully initiated member of our Church—and could receive all the Sacraments.*) An important distinction is that these "solutions" only applied to non-Christian unions, but they are a clear example of a Church declaring that it has power over matrimony. Power that, in my opinion, the Church is entirely too hesitant to utilize, allowing millions to stumble forward, desperately trying to hold on to their faith without the gift of the Eucharist.

What's the difference between these solutions and annulment? An annulment—and they occur frequently today—is the declaration by a Church matrimonial tribunal that *the marriage was invalid from the beginning*. In contrast, the two privileges don't address any validity of the previous marriage, because it was a non-Christian marriage (and therefore outside the Sacraments and therefore not "valid" to begin with in the eyes of the Church). If the Church could find solutions to failed marriages in the second century, shouldn't it try to do so in the 21st?

If anyone has been involved with divorce, or knows someone who has (and we all have), you know that the separation, which is entered into for the purposes of solving a problem, frequently generates many new problems. There are children growing up in two families, and if there are subsequent marriages, growing up with stepparents, with conflicting personalities, and all of the other baggage that can come with this situation.

Nevertheless, it's frequently necessary for a couple to part company. When I was counseling married couples, I always did what the Church wanted me to do—namely, I tried to expend every possible effort and take every possible approach to salvage the marriage. Happily, this frequently resulted in a good, productive outcome. Sometimes, however, it was simply impossible. When that point had been reached, I would urge the couple to proceed with a divorce, but to try and make it as fair and open and honest as possible. The prime reason for this is that if children were produced from that marriage, that couple will still be involved with each other for years and years to come.

That snap of a gavel by a domestic court judge, with the expression, "Divorce granted," *does not bring that relationship completely to an end*. The two families will interact over business matters, property, shared vacations with the children, and ultimately, attending their children's weddings and other social events. Be fair, be friendly, be open, be generous, and be Christian.

Let's go back to the tragedy of divorce itself. The causes are numerous, but a few can be picked out and shown to be the cause for most divorces. The reasons are rather obvious. The important thing to do when couples are beginning to date is to look for the danger signs, and to make sure they are not present in this particular couple's relationship.

The most important single virtue that should be had by both parties is maturity. Maturity interlocks with generosity. If both the young man and young woman have a reasonable amount of maturity (which calls for generosity), then that marriage is almost assured of being successful.

There are other factors that can hurt a marriage. One is difference in religion. Yes, we all have some friends who have different religions and still have successful marriages, but frankly, I think it is a handicap. Perhaps it's because of generosity and maturity that these rare couples are able to sustain the marriage. When you don't have similar beliefs as to what life is all about, when you don't share the same belief about how life should be lived, it's a real burden.

I hate to say it, but finances are a tremendous cause of discord in a marriage. There is a certain amount of money and independence that a couple must have if they are going to have children and raise those children. If there is a lack of money because of a deficiency in education or work ethic, then that's a huge problem. I shouldn't really have to stress that, because if you have maturity, then the work ethic is going to be there. In our society, you have to be productive. There is no free lunch. If you're mature, you're simply going to go to work—they go together.

Another aspect of maturity is that you should not marry someone that you don't know. That sounds silly, doesn't it? But it's very important. In interviewing young couples in preparation for marriage, I'd always ask the groom, and later the bride (in confidence), to tell me the greatest weakness of their potential spouse. I laugh now, because the person asked would very often say, "She's wonderful!" or, "He's terrific!" If that was all they said, I'd throw my pen across the desk and say, "Get somebody else to witness your marriage, because I can't in good conscience witness it when you obviously don't know Bill (or Mary), because he or she is a human being with flaws and weaknesses, and maybe one or two of them are quite serious!" If you don't know those weaknesses, and you marry him or her, you are going to have huge challenges being committed until death do you part.

So, the important message is that parents must teach their children to adjust to reality. Don't let them think that "I want" can easily be translated into "I have."

Teach them to share, to put up with others. Teach them to watch the television station that the other person in the room wants to watch sometimes. Little sacrifices are just that- little; yet they make a big difference.

Parents want many good things for their kids. They want their children to grow up with good teeth. They want their children to be educated well enough to cope in our society. I believe that the greatest single concern for parents when they are raising their children should be to raise young men and young women who will make *extraordinary husbands and wives*, who will be generous and productive fathers and mothers, and who will be major contributors to a better world. I think the best way to do this is by both of you demonstrating (in words and in deeds) a mature, generous, healthy adult relationship for your children to emulate, *whether or not you are able to remain married.*

THE RESTLESS EVIL

"If anyone does not stumble in what he says, he is a perfect man, able to bridle the whole body as well. Now, if we put the bits into the horses' mouths so that they may obey us, we direct their entire body as well.

"So also the tongue is only a small part of the body, and yet it boasts of great things. The tongue is a restless evil and full of deadly poison."
—*James 3: 2-8*

One of the most interesting things about human nature is our powerful interest in *"the story."* When you stop to think about it, books, movies, and virtually every form of communication that people utilize is built around "the story." What happened? Who did it? Where did it happen? Why did it happen, and what was the outcome? We love stories.

What are the stories about? Nobody does a story about a landslide unless people are in front of it. Nobody tells a story about a tremendous hurricane out in the Atlantic Ocean. It becomes a story when the plot involves *people*. Stories, if they are interesting, are always about people. So, the bottom line is that the most interesting thing in our lives is people, and guess what? We are people. We may be interested in science or mathematics, but when push comes to shove, we want to know "the story." That's the reason we have the great temptation to talk about other people. It's not all bad. It's completely natural, but this action can be abused.

Let me jump to using the ugly word, "gossip." The gossipmonger is the one who gossips a lot. I've always said that women gossip terribly. And do you know the only people who gossip more than women? Men. It's true!

They, of course, think they are simply "analyzing" the person's faults, and that it's all very scientific.

The vast majority of conversations about other people—usually people who are not there—are harmless. It's very natural, and we're interested in what's going on in other people's lives, what's happening to them, and we talk about it.

Gossip in the strict sense is not that kind of harmless chatter. Gossip is talking negatively about people—the weaknesses we perceive them to have, or what we think are the limitations or failures of those with whom we are sharing life. What we say can be true or false, but in either case, it's destructive. I want to stress the fact that something true—perhaps something negative about that person—doesn't make it all right to discuss. Gossip is a sin against the eighth commandment: *thou shalt not bear false witness against a neighbor.*

Implicit in that commandment is the right of every person to have a good name.

If we reveal negative facts about people, *even if they're true*, we are taking their name away from them. If they have done evil deeds in a very public manner, it's not the sin of gossip, but more the sin of uncharitableness. For example, here's someone with a good reputation, and I find out that he used to be addicted to cocaine a few years earlier. Do other people have a right to know that? No. (Okay, if you're a counselor helping people rehabilitate from cocaine, you might need to know, but the general public doesn't need to know.) Informing other people about that problem is gossip, and it's morally wrong. The fact that it's accurate information does not justify spreading the information.

It's a different situation when you read about someone's mistakes on the front page of the paper. Their reputation, at least in that one area, is badly damaged, and assuming the news is true, it is their fault. ***However, we ought not to make it a recreation to talk about the weaknesses of other people.*** Often, we do. I think that it's important to recognize that it's an inherently human trait, and practically universal, to talk about other people. What we need to do is to discipline ourselves in two ways:

1. Try to avoid revealing negative information about other people.
2. Try to cultivate the habit of saying positive things about people.

While we all tend to talk about other people, what we don't typically do is to focus on their good qualities. The temptation to discuss the negative is much more powerful than the temptation to discuss the positive. Therefore, we need to foster a habit within ourselves, that when a person's name comes up, we instinctively say about that person what we know that is good and positive. The problem is that sometimes, frankly, it's not as interesting! Let's work on it, anyway.

BUT ARE YOU REALLY SURE?

*"Mario, what do you get when you cross an insomniac,
an unwilling agnostic, and a dyslexic?" "I give." "You get
someone who stays up all night torturing himself mentally
over the question of whether or not there's a dog."*
— *David Foster Wallace,* Infinite Jest

An agnostic is a person who doesn't know whether or not there is a God. He's willing to shrug his shoulders and say, "You know, there may be, but nobody has ever proven His existence to me. And I know all these people who are praying that they'll win the football game, that the cure for cancer will be found, and it never happens." If He's an all-willing God, why do things turn out that way? An atheist is very different. An atheist has a firm conviction that there is no divine being.

As I look back over most of my adult years, I think of the fact that I have known very few committed agnostics. I've known a certain number of them, and I may have known others who were practical agnostics, but wouldn't say so because it's not socially acceptable in even the most vaguely Christian environments, which is where most of us live. But I have to ask myself, why aren't there MORE agnostics?

The things that we believe can't be seen, and can't be proven. It seems to me that the vast majority of the intelligent adults of our society ought to be agnostic, or at least give serious consideration to being agnostic. Why is that? We instinctively demand truth, and most humans demand the physical proof before they believe in something.

Let's take a concrete example. "The bus will be here in twenty minutes." How do you know that? Have you been here before? Have you caught the bus before? Who told you that? Do you have a printed schedule?

We challenge everything, and that's how we learn. So, challenging concepts that are placed in front of us is very, very natural. Therefore, there's nothing wrong with being an agnostic. In fact, I consider it to be the natural state.

Now, the reverse of that is that we have a desperate desire for meaning, and for answers. The human mind will not accept "uncaused causes" (that's a philosophical term).

Another example: The mother comes home. The seven-year-old boy has been in the house by himself for about fifteen minutes, and she comes back into the house. In the middle of the living room carpet, a can of soda has been spilled. The mother says, "What happened?" The boy says, "I don't know. It just appeared there." The mother's mind will not allow her to accept that, and she is doing something that's tremendously important philosophically. She innately understands causality—that nothing just happens by itself.

So, over here on the left, we've got the agnostics who are looking around for meaning, and don't find proof. And over here on the right, we have people of faith, who also look for meaning and do find proof. They say that to them the universe—or more properly now, the totality of creation—is so awesome that we can't begin to grasp the enormity of it. If the mother can't accept the ink spot in the middle of the rug as "just happening," then why should the man of faith accept that all of this awesome, intricate reality just happened or just evolved? There's nothing wrong with evolution, but you're going from cause to causality. I think it works out in most people's lives.

There's a potential conflict between the desire for absolute proof and the desire for meaning. Therefore, this conflict exists in nearly everyone between faith and agnosticism. Most people will resolve that conflict on the basis of meaning, which means they will become people of faith. People that they have respected—their parents, their teachers, religious leaders, sacred authors—have been for thousands and thousands of years providing a fairly consistent explanation for the existence that we see around us, and that fairly consistent explanation calls for a being that is "uncaused." That's the philosophical explanation of God: the uncaused cause which has no beginning.

Of course, the mind has to wrestle with that: no beginning. I don't know what that means. I can say those words, but I don't know what that means. But that's a better explanation for the vast majority of people than the agnostic who says there is no proof of God, but still ends up with no explanation for anything. Let me repeat that: the agnostic has no explanation and no Divine Being to whom he should direct some respect and adoration; whereas the believing person has an explanation just as meaningful as the agnostic's denial, and at the same time has the consolation of slipping back into something comfortable and secure. Ultimately, I think that everyone has the potential toward agnosticism, but the vast majority of people choose not to go down that road.

A few years ago, an 18-month-old baby fell down a well, nearly 200 feet. They dug a companion hole and took two days to get to the baby, and when they did, the baby was dead. When something so tragic as this happens, we all question, how can there be a loving God? And this kind of story will produce that reaction over and over when people think about it a great deal. Interestingly, though—some people's faith grows stronger in the midst of difficulty and pain.

When you go back in time to the beginning of the world, there is no proof of what happened. Agnostics have no proof and no answer. People of faith have no proof, but at least they do have an answer. In either case, you are not going to get clear precise answers.

What should you do if you have a friend who is an agnostic? My advice is to let them be. I literally have not had an argument over religion in more than forty years. Why? It's a complete waste of time to argue with someone over any aspect of religion. I can tell you what I believe—that's all I can do. You do with that what you want. If you want to think it's crazy, that's fine. It's a free country. I tell agnostics that they have a perfectly logical position. Nobody can prove that there's a God, especially a God who interferes in our lives. And we Catholics don't just believe in God. In fact, the Jews and the Christians and the Mohammadans, we believe that God's *involved* in our story. Other faiths—Hindus, etc.—believe in gods, but they don't see them as being involved in day-to-day living.

Anyway, agnostics have a perfectly logical position. I don't espouse it—I have a very different point of view—but I would never ever try to argue with a person about their beliefs. I can and will give you the reasons I believe, but they would not necessarily motivate you to come around to my way of thinking.

WHAT ABOUT HOMOSEXUALITY?

Q: What do you think of when you consider the issue of homosexuality?

Speaking just for myself, my initial reaction is a feeling of sadness, because often there is so much pain involved. In the United States today, there is a tremendous internal conflict over the subject of homosexuality. Numbers and statistics really have nothing to do with the issue, per se, but we might want to factor it into our discussion. Some students of the subject contend that only about 3-5% of our population is actually homosexual. Others within the gay community contend that it might rise to as high as 20 or 25%. Since there is so much opprobrium over the issue, I'd imagine that a large percentage of men and women who are actually gay still choose to live a life "in the closet." This means that they must live a public life separated in most respects from their real inner self.

The present tension in the United States is due to the fact that the gay community has come to realize that virtually every other minority segment of our society has fought fairly successful battles to achieve near-equality in American life. The gay community has been waging that struggle for many years now, with a considerable degree of success.

The principle battleground today is the issue of gay marriage. The gay community wants their unions to be treated as equal to marriages among heterosexual couples. The division across the country is very sharp and bitter. A number of states now recognize gay marriage, and a sizable number have changed their state constitutions from prohibiting it. In this area, I am at odds with the administrative posture of the Church in the United States. So far, as this issue surfaces in individual states, the Church has attempted to marshal its rather sizable resources to defeat any effort at bringing about a change. To me the issue is simple. *The Church believes that marriage between two baptized persons is a sacrament, and the Church holds strongly that this Sacrament can be received and celebrated only between a man and a woman.* The state and civil society has a broader reach, and must pass laws for every citizen. I personally see no reason why committed homosexual couples should not enjoy the same legal and tax benefits as committed heterosexual couples. The Church governs and controls the Sacraments, not civil society. Where do we go from here?

We can look at this issue from two perspectives. One is its relationship to our whole society. Those persons burdened with this condition are struggling to be treated as American citizens, with the same rights and duties of all other citizens in the country. A number of powerful groups, such as the moral majority, are endeavoring to keep them from doing that. My guess is that as this issue moves forward in the courts, it will be resolved there, and resolved in a way that will protect the rights of gay persons.

I personally consider homosexuality to be a very serious burden on anyone who finds him- or herself cast in this role in our society. To be fair, I am not gay, so I acknowledge that I cannot fully appreciate all of the emotions and issues that homosexual people must face. Additionally, I will admit that my own attitudes about homosexuality have gradually evolved over the years, partially reflecting the increasing societal awareness. However, I do have a fair amount of experience with young men and women who have accepted the fact that they are gay. I, as of yet, know of no one in that condition who is enthusiastic about that discovery. Why? Because this realization entails either a hidden life, or choosing to live a life facing frequent disdain and hostility.

The Church's directions for homosexuals are very inadequate. The Church properly says that being a homosexual is *not sinful.* Of course, how could it be? That's the person's inner nature. However, the Church goes on to say that that person, once they realize they are gay, can never enter into a morally acceptable sexual relationship with a person of the same sex.

Through the centuries, the Church has honored and paid tribute to men and women who freely chose to lead celibate lives. They have often been placed on a pedestal for this choice. What about the 19-year-old boy or 20-year-old girl who has come to grips with his or her homosexuality? They do not feel they have a vocation to celibacy. They have the same strong sexual drives as any other normal human being, and yet they are told those drives cannot be satisfied. The Church is actually saying that if you are gay, you are called to celibacy. Why did they decide that? Not a good choice, in my humble opinion.

Every individual who accepts the reality of his or her homosexuality has to endeavor to live their lives as best they can. I have a particularly special place in my heart for the parents of gay and lesbian children. As our society becomes more sensitive to the complexity of the issue, the burden that parents carry is happily lighter than it would have been two generations ago. However, at the most natural level, these parents realize they will never have the joy of seeing grandchildren naturally born of those children. Yes, there are potentially alternative family options, but it is not quite the same as seeing the children of your children.

One of the common issues in this circumstance is that many parents suffer from a tragically misguided sense of guilt. "Where did I fail?" they wonder. "What did I do wrong?" The answer should be sure and direct: your child is not gay because of anything you did. What you need to do now is to surround them with intense love and support, which is an extraordinary practice of Christian virtue.

I don't believe anyone chooses homosexuality. I believe it a present in a person's life from conception. And let me say again that I believe it is almost invariably a burden, not only to the individual, but also to their family and friends (as they watch their loved one deal with societal hostility and judgment). If the person involved has not chosen to be homosexual, and if that person does not feel called to celibacy, what are they to do? I do not expect to see the Church change its position.

This leaves us with a very difficult situation. *What can we do?* As a Catholic priest, I cannot contradict the formal teaching of our Church, but I *can* call for a major surge in sensitivity, empathy, generosity, and patience. No one should add to the burden that is already very real and very present.

None of us should add to pain in other people's lives. Thanks be to God that we live in a nation that protects extraordinary differences in religion, value systems, lifestyles, and sexuality. Let's do the same.

HERE COMES THE BRIDE

"It's easier to be buried than married!"
—Bishop John McCarthy

The heart of religious life, the life of faith in the Catholic Church, centers on the Sacraments. Catholics believe that the seven holy symbols that the Church uses in celebrating the sacraments are sacred signs that bring us into direct contact with Jesus of Nazareth. The faithful and the Savior reach towards each other and are joined in the sacramental life of the church.

These seven sacred signs of our spiritual life closely parallel the major events in our natural life as we live out our years on this planet. Baptism relates to rebirth, and the Eucharist is spiritual food. All of the Sacraments are extremely important, but I would like to focus on one of the sacraments that has tremendous ramifications for the people living their lives in the Church. I am referring to **matrimony.**

The majority of people in the Church receive this sacrament, and ordinarily it is only to be received once. The teachings of Jesus and St. Paul are clear about the importance of monogamous marriages and their permanence, but over the centuries, the Church has added many extras to the sacramental reality that is matrimony.

I would like to see young couples come out of the church office filled with exuberance after making the initial contact to schedule their wedding in their parish church. I'm sad to say that many times this is not the case. Often, after visiting the church office and jubilantly announcing their love for each other—which they want to see blessed and joined by the sacrament of matrimony—young couples find themselves turned off by the church secretary whose first question is, "Are you registered in the parish?"

and follows the question with a list of conditions for the ceremony which may or may not be easily fulfilled by this young couple.

I understand that at this time, with a serious shortage of priests, some parishes are staffed with only one priest to serve thousands of parishioners, and it's necessary to use office staff to handle the logistical side of this issue. But such staff workers need to be sensitized to the negative effects that follow from responding to a jubilant expression of joy and love with cold, canonical questions.

We can go farther with that, but let me give you some ideas. Is there a wedding pending in your family or in that of a friend? There are a few suggestions, which might help you prepare for that wedding and help you avoid any misunderstandings at the time of the rehearsal, wedding, or reception. All aspects of the festivities may become dangerous fields loaded with landmines!

Here are a few ways to simplify your wedding arrangements. First, the normal place for a Catholic wedding is in the parish of the bride. If you're going to go there, it's very important that you be registered. Many young couples say they go there every week, but are not registered, and so the church office has not heard of them. Of course, the church office should be just as kind to that couple as to one that has been active in the parish— but the temptation is to be distant and resentful. Think about it from the standpoint of the office staff. Don't surface just when you want to borrow a four-million-dollar church for a few hours! (And yes, that is the worth of an average parish church.)

Secondly, because of the rampant divorce in our society, most dioceses have erected a braking mechanism to prevent young people from getting married after a wildly successful Saturday night date. Most parishes, therefore, will ask very quickly how long you have known each other, and whether you can wait six months to get married. In other words, from the day of registration with the church, six months must pass. This is very offensive to young couples, but is also often a Godsend that avoids painful mistakes that can last a lifetime.

You will need to bring a certain amount of bureaucratic information that you won't be told about until you attempt to schedule your wedding. What an impression you would create in your home rectory if you walked in with copies of your baptismal certificate and proof that neither has been married (this is the "free state form"—a form filled out by someone, typically a parent or other relative, who is able to testify that neither of you has had a prior wedding).

Let me tell you, when there has been a prior wedding, things immediately get very complicated. This is all the more reason to open a conversation with your priest, deacon, or sensitive secretary as soon as possible. It may sound complicated, but everything can be worked out, and it's important that you move into this period of planning with a focus on accenting your love for each other rather than being made unnecessarily angry by red tape and bureaucracy within the Church.

Let's move on to the wedding itself. At most weddings, there are two dangerous people present: the bride herself, and the MOTB (mother of the bride). Well in advance of the wedding, these two important people must realize that in an important, complex event such as a wedding day, things can and often do go wrong. Modern air conditioners are designed only to fail on Saturday afternoons! I have seen wedding dresses and very expensive flowers delivered to the wrong church. At the moment it's heartbreaking, but to more mature people it will often be funny five years later.

Now, the reception: what was said about possible mix-ups for weddings is true for receptions as well. One sensitive area that we often don't talk about is that in America today, we sometimes find ourselves attending weddings of young people whose parents are divorced and remarried. *Extreme sensitivity is required to pass through this particular minefield without any unpleasant developments!* I've been at many receptions where these former families, now reunited, are more focused on each other than the happy couple. They avoid each other to the point of creating unhappy tension in a day that should be joyous.

As an aside- for years, I tried to get young couples to consider planning their weddings at the same time that weddings were scheduled fifty years ago—10am and noon—because all that was required was a cookie-and-punch reception, and the couple would be on their way without much exhaustion or extraordinary expense. I don't believe I've ever convinced anyone to do this, but I'll continue to suggest it.

Marriage is a blessing from God, but sometimes events at weddings can tempt our faith. Have a sense of humor! Concentrate on your love for your fiancé. Remember that it is your wedding, not your parents' or siblings' wedding. Take a long honeymoon afterward, and return refreshed, ready to start the real work of sharing life together.

'TILL DEATH DO US PART

*"How can a priest give marital advice, when he has
never been married?"*
—*Bishop John McCarthy*

It should come as no surprise that I have never been married, and I believe
any chance of that happening in the near future is limited, at best. However,
in my role as a parish priest, I have spent endless hours consulting with
couples that are struggling to maintain a relationship that began in love
and faith, but subsequently appear to be in grave danger. While hopefully
the majority (or at least, very many) married couples are doing completely
fine, a clergyman's view of marriage is often skewed towards recognizing
those in trouble, as that is who comes to seek our counsel. I'd like to be
clear that in counseling couples, I would make every possible effort to save
their union, but in those cases where it was truly impossible and divorce
was eminent, I would always petition them to attempt to go through that
painful process with as little bitterness or destructiveness as possible. Sadly,
this is not always successful.

Every marital relationship is obviously unique, because each individual is a distinctive human being with different motivations and desires.
Nevertheless, there is a certain commonality that seems to surface in struggling marriages. I consider three issues to be the most common causes
for marriage breakdown and dissolution: The first is ignorance of the
true nature of the spouse. The second reason boils down to having a low
threshold for pain. Finally, the third is the very basic issue of pure financial
inadequacy.

Let's talk first about knowing the true nature of your spouse. Throughout my entire life as a parish priest, I never witnessed a marriage without first inquiring of the bride and the groom what was the greatest attraction to their fiancé. It pains me to say this, but frequently I would hear the response that she was "so beautiful" or he was "a divine dancer." Naturally, I was hoping (and most of the time I received) wonderful answers such as "he is strong, mature and generous," or "she is honest, caring of her family and faithful to her friends." ***These marvelous qualities reflect the real person that is there.*** Our marriage prep courses were designed to help couples get to know each other more profoundly, and to have deeper insight into the character of their fiancé. Quite frankly, we would sometimes feel sadly relieved to hear that a particular couple broke up after completing the course. How much better to discover the incompatibility *before* the vows are taken… What happens when this revelation occurs two or three years later, often with a baby or two now included? People "wake up" and realize they simply don't know each other- maybe don't really even like each other- and they end up divorced.

The second issue involves what I refer to as "a low threshold for pain". Life is hard- it comes with many discomforts, inconveniences and "pain." *Life sharing* is always a challenge. Note that I did not say life sharing is *frequently* a challenge, but **ALWAYS** a challenge. How can we rise to this challenge? Everyone needs to develop *virtues* (which, by the way, simply means "good habits") in order to share life with another person. Virtues make sharing life not only possible, but even potentially joyful. Which virtues do you need for a successful marriage? An easy answer! First of all, maturity. **Maturity is** defined by John McCarthy as **the ability to adjust to reality**. The second most important virtue is generosity, the gift that enables us to live not WITH but FOR other people. Couples who focus on practicing these virtues will find that they have an enormous "threshold for pain," thus tremendously increasing their odds for a fruitful marriage. Throw in developing your sense of humor, and now you've truly got a recipe for success.

The last issue is finances. This is an easy one, because finances are simple- you've got to have money. Money allows for food, shelter, and other basic needs. In fairness, both parties should determine what financial base is necessary for their emotional and physical comfort-which certainly varies from person to person. Is it enough for simple groceries on the table, or gourmet restaurants? Regardless of the absolute dollar amount, an inadequate financial base for the family means agonizing insecurity, for both the husband and the wife. From that insecurity comes disappointment and anger, and those vices have the potential to undercut any marriage.

IS IT TIME TO DIE?

"Death is a much more complicated situation today than it was fifty years ago, because medical advances have made it so easy to keep people alive."
—*Bishop John McCarthy*

You don't have to live many years on this planet before you recognize the fact that you have come face to face with death. Maybe it was the death of a distant relative. Maybe it was the tragically untimely death of a student in your high school. Whatever it was, it caused you to stare into the mystery of life and death, and to attempt to come to grips with the idea that our lives on this planet are not going to go on forever. We're all going to die.

As the years roll by, we have more and more experience of the reality of death. If we're honest, we note that these experiences somehow seem to get closer and closer to us as we get older. A young person may have someone close to them who is dying, but it happens more often to someone who is fifty or sixty years old. Is it advanced cancer? There's not really much you can do about that. Is it a person who is injured badly in a car accident and not expected to live? You can do whatever is possible in terms of the hospital situation, but really, no one can actually control this. Did the person commit suicide? Then they're simply just gone.

In some sense, those types of unalterable situations represent how many of us end life on this planet. But a new situation has developed in the last two or three decades. The tremendous advances in medicine and the awesome power of the medical community have given us power over the life of a dying person. We now have the technical competence to extend a person's life *almost infinitely* by normal human standards. But by forcing someone's body to breathe with a ventilator, accept fluids from intravenous lines (IV hydration), and forcing nutrition into their body via tubes, you're extending that person's life beyond what it was meant to be. Let me be clear, there's no moral obligation to do that.

Life is a great gift. We should maintain it as long as we can. But dying is natural, just like being born is natural. And when a person is approaching death *and no benefit can come from extended treatment*, great and unnecessary problems can be created by trying everything to keep them alive. There's a tremendous financial cost involved in keeping somebody in an extended care facility for six weeks, or six months, or a year. A family's finances can be totally wiped out.

We all die. We are born and we die, and they are always connected, sooner or later. And life is a wonderful gift that should be respected and enhanced to the extent that anybody can do that. But when the situation comes—as it comes to everyone—that death is approaching, then certain decisions have to be made.

One question that can help you reach that decision is, "Will this treatment allow the person to continue a life that has some kind of quality? Is there something they still enjoy about life?" There are many ways that life can be defined. And I, personally, would not define "life" as being pumped up with food and air. That's not a life, and, again, there is no obligation to do that.

If the medical world stepped back and just focused on easing pain, a person who is sick or injured might die in one to two weeks. However, that same group of medical personnel can now potentially keep that same person alive for months or years. Sometimes that means keeping the person alive with a tragic amount of pain, and tremendous additional burdens being endured by the family.

The Church teaches that all life is sacred and must be protected, and that a person should ordinarily live until some disease or accident beyond their control takes their lives. But what about the person who is definitely dying, has no possible hope of recovery, and is in pain and costing $6,000 per day to be kept alive?

I personally agree with Pope Pius XII that there is no obligation to extend the dying process. What do I mean by that? Very specifically, I mean that if a person is definitely dying anyway, and medicine might postpone that death a day or a week, there is no obligation to extend the dying process, so that medicine does not necessarily need to be given—it is not obligatory. *I say this in the face of a statement by Pope John Paul II that holds the opposite positio*n.

However, we have always had the principle that there is no obligation to extend a person's life artificially. Forcing a man to breathe with a machine, and forcing nutrition into his body with a tube is artificial. But in a rather casual speech in the last two years of his life, Pope John Paul II said, "Breathing and eating..." (hydration and nutrition) "...is not special. It's natural. You must take care of a dying person as long as you possibly can."

It wasn't an official statement. It was just made to a relatively small group, but it's caused a tremendous ruckus because that statement turned into being a position of the Church. *Just a casual remark like that by the Pope can have huge ramifications.* I believe that's one of the changes we have to make.

I think that God gave us horse sense and logic, and when nothing is to be gained for the patient other than an extended process of dying, *and* great harm is being done to the family, then we should make our decisions based on what causes the least amount of pain and the most good.

When I was a kid, the Church was constantly encouraging us to pray for a happy death. I think an impending death, virtually free of pain, and not overly extended, would be a happy death.

OUR FINAL HOME

*"Dying is natural, like being born is natural.... The Irish consider
death a solution, not a problem. We go for death. We have
big celebrations. We really do."*
—Bishop John McCarthy

When a person is mature enough to really look at his or her life, and tries
to prioritize and evaluate each and every aspect of it, it's not long before
the reality of death presents itself. Everybody has to face it; everybody must
confront the reality that we will not live on this planet forever. In fact, we're
here on this planet for a relatively short time, whether we die at age 3 or
102. The fact is that we react to this reality in many, many different ways.

One of the most common reactions is a strong desire on the part of
many people, whether they are twenty or sixty, to simply not face it. They
don't want to deal with death. I consider this a big mistake. It's so real.
It's the only single thing we can be absolutely certain of. We are going to
die. Therefore, how we die—how we prepare for dying, what we expect of
it—is of tremendous importance. To not think about death and not talk
about it, to not pray over death and factor it in as a major component and
guidance about the way we live, is a terrible mistake.

I don't think there has been any period in history where we've had so
many resources to help with the potential fears surrounding the process of
dying. The pain of dying to a great extent has been lessened. Palliative care
can ease the transition tremendously. We simply don't have to dread the
prospect of a painful death the way we used to.

We do, however, have to worry about prolonging death- merely keeping a body going. Frankly people died more quickly years ago. Disease

made people sick. There weren't medical resources available to keep them alive. The Church says that death is as natural as birth. There is no obligation to extend life with extraordinary measures, like ventilators and forced feeding.

At any rate, why do people avoid facing the reality of death? Men and women of faith should be able to approach death and dying with a great deal of calmness. I don't have the slightest dread about being dead, even though I am concerned about the dying process. Death is sort of simple: it's over. Dying, however, can be long and drawn out. It can be painful for us. It can be taxing for the people that love us. If we're just dreading the closing-out phase, that's understandable. If it's dreading the end of our existence on this planet, for people of faith it should instead be a source of encouragement.

I believe I was created by a God who loves me and wants me to exist. That's one of the most thrilling things a person can imagine! God wanted me here. God wanted *you* here. *God wants us here.* Life flows because He has an infinite love for each and all of us. Death is simply the point in our story when the earthly struggle ends, and eternal joy begins. For a believer in the Christian faith, it should be an extraordinarily positive thought. And yet, we don't want to face it. I say, come to grips with the fact that you've less time to live than you did last week. Come to grips to the fact that your body is a little bit weaker than it was two years ago. Reap joy, and pride, and optimism from those facts.

Of course, that's easier said than done. Death is the great unknown, and that's what frightens us.

Suppose the Christian story is not true. Suppose the God that we worship is not as loving as we think. Suppose He's the cruel taskmaster that some phases of Christianity have made Him, and He's waiting to catch us in some grave sin and send us off to eternal suffering. For the person who thinks that way, death can absolutely be fearful. But in my opinion, that doesn't reflect a solid Christian faith. Christian faith is a joyful thing—we believe that the God who created us and sustains us loves us.

Why should we not, then, look forward to death? Well, it's in our nature to really love being alive, to love being here. Now, there are people in difficult circumstances—like people in jail, or in filthy conditions— they don't enjoy life. In general, though, people enjoy being alive, and it's reflected in their struggle to stay alive. Yes, there are suicides, and people who willingly give their lives for other people, but the vast majority of us want to live. Theologically, this innate desire to live is a reflection of the fact that we are created for eternal life. There is the love of being alive today, and the openness to eternal life hereafter.

One should not fear death. One should not fear that which is real. One should not fear that which cannot be avoided. We need to learn to handle it—to handle it while we're young and healthy and vigorous, and to handle it when we're older and weak and dependent. We must know that it's coming, that death is a gateway or entryway to nothing but an unbelievably eternal, wonderful existence. Instead of seeing death and the dark shadows of our lives as the Grim Reaper, we should see an angel sent from God, or perhaps God, Himself, reaching out with His arms to embrace us and call us home—the home for which we were created. Our final home is going to be magnificent.

While I have always tried to stress the beautiful and joyous aspects of ending this life and entering eternal life, I do want to say something critical about Christian funerals. I believe that the simple act of disposing of the remains of a loved one should be surrounded with faith, prayerfulness, calmness and acceptance of reality. But those important factors should not cost a fortune, nor financially handicap a family that is handling the responsibilities. Funeral homes understandably are in business to make money, and many of them will endeavor to sell as much of their product as they can. Families with limited means should resist that, and utilize their finite resources for those who continue to struggle on this earth.

One other issue is that older people may be still sometimes shocked with the rapidly spreading use of cremation. If you are seventy-five years old, you would have a clear memory that not only was cremation forbidden by the Catholic Church, *but the parish would refuse to even conduct the services for the person cremated*. In reality, cremation had only been banned from the Church since the 1700s. At any rate, that concept disappeared in the 1960s when the bishops of the second Vatican council got their memories refreshed. Cremation was forbidden by Church law prior to 1965 primarily because of an old tradition that people who were bitterly anti-Christian and did not believe in eternal life would have their remains cremated as a final insult to Christian faith. They thought that somehow

God was limited to what He could do after death. They thought ashes would symbolize that it was all over. Many of the leaders of this point of view were anti-Catholic Freemasons. This perspective has long since disappeared. I want to be clear that cremation is no longer prohibited in the Catholic Church, and this choice is becoming much more common in Catholic funeral services.

THE BIGGEST DECISION
A MOTHER MAKES

*"Let the one among you who is guiltless be the
first to throw a stone."*
—*John 8:7*

*"Our God offers hope to all. Even those women who have been violated
by abortion can find peace and healing through forgiveness and
reconciliation through the Church."*
—*Bishop John McCarthy*

Within an individual human family, one of the strongest forces is love. At
the natural level, love is the mortar that holds us together. Husbands and
wives, parents and children, and even siblings and distant relatives and
friends are bound together not by geographic proximity, but by the acts of
love that proceed from our will. It's love that gives us the strength to stay
together even in the face of prickly differences.

Ordinarily speaking, one might say that there are different degrees of
love within the human family. Needless to say, they can't be measured, but
the popular view is that within the family the love of a mother for her child
is extraordinarily powerful. Most of us would agree to that being true in
general. If that hypothesis is accepted, then a mother's decision to end the
life of her unborn child seems horrible and unthinkable.

The United States has acted sadly and badly on this issue since Jan 22,
1973. On that day, the Supreme Court of our country stripped the unborn
child of any legal standing, and in so doing withdrew the protections that

had been in place not merely by civil laws, but by common acceptance of a powerful law which goes under the awesome title "Natural."

The next four decades saw bitter and unending conflict over efforts to restructure the Supreme Court and bring about the restoration of protection to the unborn. The struggle has been vicious and divisive, and it goes on to this day. In the years immediately following the court's decision entitled Roe vs. Wade, the principal opponent was the Roman Catholic Church. Later, other groups joined with the Catholics, and today abortion is no longer seen as simply a Catholic issue, but rather an issue for which virtually every thoughtful citizen has an opinion. While Catholic leaders were delighted that other groups such as the Baptists and the Mormons entered the fray, the Bishops continue to be leaders in the organizational efforts to bring about change. The Church has fostered parallel organizations, such as state and national pro-life committees, which are directly involved in the political processes in a manner that the institutional sectors of the Church cannot exercise.

I have strong views on the subject. I accept totally and unconditionally the teachings of my Church surrounding the sacredness and uniqueness of every individual. I believe that life begins at the moment of conception and develops in a straight line until terminated by this or that cause. I believe that an unborn child possesses an immortal soul, and is invited to share God's life for all eternity.

Nevertheless, I take exception to the basic organizational thrust of the Catholic Church in the United States as it endeavors to counter the agonizing reality of abortion. In my opinion, the Church must take primarily a prophetic role, not a political one. The Church should stand beside a society that is in so many ways sick and deformed, and express its dismay and its discouragement that a country so wealthy and powerful as ourselves would endeavor to solve our social problems by terminating (why are we so afraid to say "kill"?) its weakest members. The Church should assert in every way possible that this policy is a major cancer in our society, and the Church should make every effort to call the larger society to a greater understanding of the value of human life, and at the same time do everything that it can to lessen the impact of abortion and its consequences.

But what does that accomplish in the Supreme Court? Nothing, as far as the Church is concerned. It's a free country, and those who wish to influence society through power politics are free to do it, but I do not believe that this should be the main thrust of the Church. I believe at this point, there is no way to overturn Roe vs. Wade, because ultimately that would involve primarily punishing scared, isolated, often teenage girls who would be affected by the law, and that will never be politically acceptable. Again, I say the Church must be prophetic in teaching and preaching, not delving into the political trenches that only deepen the divisions within the community.

The Church has long taught that there ought to be a relationship between civil law and the natural moral law, but the Church has never taught that civil or criminal penalties ought to be utilized in every situation where moral wrongdoing occurs. Muslim communities do practice this, but here in the United States, we happily do not.

Therefore, the Church would be fulfilling its mission to teach, teach, teach the truth of human life, and to pray, pray, pray for its protection in all instances, without trying to accomplish that goal by wielding the political power of the Church itself. If others are able to do that, more power to them, but I believe it should not be undertaken directly by the Church.

Why is that?

Frankly, that is not the mission of the Church.

Since I feel the Church should not be accomplishing its goals just with political muscle, I certainly also want to publicly condemn those so-called "pro-life" people who have bombed clinics and assassinated abortion doctors. Once again, this great religious family that is the Church needs to convey the sacredness of human life, but *do it by example*, conveyed through love and concern for the vulnerable members of our society.

As I've said, prayer and preaching are very important, but the best form of preaching and teaching is service to vulnerable women in our society, which of course includes both the young mother who is living through what is called a "problem pregnancy," and the unborn child itself. I want to thank and praise the tens of thousands of men and women who generously give of themselves in order to assist young mothers who find themselves in agonizing situations. Marywood and Project Rachel are prime examples of this type of organization, but there are many others operating across the country with similar goals: to reach out to frightened, often lonely, and poor women who see abortion as their only solution. Nevertheless, the amount of work that the institutional Church does in this regard is minimal in view of the vastness of its resources and its organizational network, so we need to get busy and do much more.

And now, I'd like to speak directly to all the women who have suffered through the horrific experience of having an abortion. I can do no better than to quote the words of our Lord, from the story where the woman caught in adultery was brought before Jesus (and where, my friends, was the man?): "Neither do I condemn you. Go away and from this moment, sin no more."

WE CAN'T AFFORD ANOTHER ONE

Q: "Bishop McCarthy, what are your thoughts on birth control?"
A: "Birth control? No problem! I've been practicing birth control for decades!"
(Priests take a vow of celibacy when they are ordained.)

The teachings of the Catholic Church regarding birth control in general, and contraception in particular, are at the center of one of the most controversial aspects of modern Catholic discussion, and are very significant issues in terms of the Church's relationship to other religious entities. I should state at the start that the Church teaches that it is not absolutely against the control of births. The Church would assert that She has always recognized various forms of birth control, but there are many contraceptive choices in today's world that the Church teaches are a distortion of nature, and therefore, immoral.

I suppose the first form of birth control, one that the Church has always accepted, is celibacy. One must admit, however, that it is not an extraordinarily popular method, although it has been used in every century during the life of the Church. Additionally, the Church has honored and extolled those who chose this life if they were embracing it, as Jesus said, for a "heavenly cause."

In the 20th century, the Church broadened its acceptance of birth control by enthusiastically embracing what it calls "natural family planning," which involves following a woman's ovulation cycle and employing periodic abstinence. This method, endorsed and aggressively fostered by the Church, is (I am told) used by large numbers of Roman Catholics. Natural family planning requires much discipline, and miscalculations can certainly occur. For these and other reasons, this method is, therefore, not universally accepted with enthusiasm by all Catholic families.

There are a number of forms of contraception widely used in today's society.

Accurate statistics are not easily available. *How many married Catholic couples actually use condoms or have the woman take a contraceptive pill?* These forms of birth control are universally condemned in the formal teachings of the Catholic Church.

What to do?

Modern industrial life has made the most essential component of family life a more demanding issue than has probably ever been the case in human history. In ages past, because of limited medical knowledge, a very large number of babies conceived were not carried to term. Even when they were carried to term, tragically many babies and their mothers died during childbirth. This reality caused the populations of villages, towns, and even whole countries to grow very slowly. In 1800, London was the only city in the world with a population of one million. Today there are over fifty cities in China alone with populations exceeding several million. This rapid increase in population has created problems at the national level as countries struggle to increase the number and amount of resources necessary to support their rapidly growing populations. If that is true for nations, it is even more accurate for families.

In 1850, when a woman told her husband, "Darling, I think we're going to have a baby!", he might have been happy; but if he were thought-ful, he might also have known that there was a good chance the baby might not make it to term, and if it did, the baby and/or the mother could die.

Today the situation is dramatically different. When the woman's counterpart in 2013 says, "Darling, we're going to have a baby," the somewhat surprised father thinks not about the latent dangers that used to lie ahead in that situation, but perhaps the fact that he just picked up the cost of a college education eighteen years hence. In 1850, when he got this information, a living healthy child was seen immediately as a blessing in every manner. The financial cost of delivery was minimal—sometimes absolutely nothing. And that little child, by the time she was three, could help feed the chickens. A boy by age four might help gather firewood. Even young children were an economic advantage on the farm. Now, this is certainly not to say that children are no longer a blessing, but to emphasize the additional financial stresses now inherent as the family expands. Today, families living in apartments, small houses and multi-story buildings have little or no benefit from their developing children in a strictly economic sense.

This brings up the global question of space. As the world's populated centers grow larger, the living area for families is smaller. Anyone familiar with the reality of New York City is aware of that.

Again, what to do?

There are many in the Catholic Church, theologians and laity, who have been uncomfortably and strongly opposed to the traditional teaching regarding the Church's stand against any mechanical or unnatural contraception. Fifty years ago, there was a growing movement to get the Church to reconsider her position. Acquiescing to the reality of that pressure, Pope Paul VI established a special commission regarding the moral aspects of contraception. The commission consisted of roughly fifty members, including medical people, scientists, and theologians drawn from across the Catholic world. They met off and on for several years, and eventually presented their decision to the Pope. *The commission unanimously endorsed the need for the Church to re-evaluate its position on contraception.*

Pope Paul VI was in agony, caught in a bind between the views of the commission (believed to reflect the views of most married Catholics at that time) and the doctrine defined in 1870 that the Bishop of Rome was infallible on subjects such as this. Earlier pontiffs had made clear and direct statements on the subject of contraception that were considered to be formal teaching by the Pope, exercising his office as the Bishop of Rome and Pastor of the universal Church. Therefore, if Pope Paul VI contradicted these statements (by following the commission's recommendation), *he would be undercutting the doctrine of papal infallibility.* Pope Paul VI could not go against that, although I'm sure he suffered through this decision.

He chose to stand by infallibility.

And once again, what to do?

Let's push aside worldwide statistics and complex arguments and moral theology. Let's push aside papal teaching and other aspects of this awesomely important issue, and look at one concrete case.

Jose is a twenty-three-year-old Hispanic laborer in East Houston. He has been married for four years, and he and his wife have been blessed with three children, though they had only planned for two. As an unskilled worker from Mexico, he can only afford a small, three-room box of a house. The economic contraction has caused his company to fold, and now he is out of a job. His wife comes home from the clinic with the terrible news that she has been diagnosed with leukemia and needs to start chemotherapy. Needless to say, the doctor suggested birth control, as it would be medically dangerous to conceive at this time. What are Jose and Maria to do? They are very poor, deeply in love, scared, lacking resources, and are terribly afraid of another pregnancy. Would this young couple, so much in love and faced with so many risks, be guilty of *immorality* if they used contraception?

My own view, and I believe that the vast majority of Catholics in the United States share this view, is that the couple *would not* be guilty of any immorality. I know that I have used by way of an example an extreme case, but I think it shows that the application of the Church's desire for "complete naturalness" has to be evaluated within a context, and not as a misuse of plumbing.

The reality is that the Catholic Church is teaching a moral position which is of extreme importance to every married person throughout their childbearing years. *The vast majority of lay Catholics have overwhelmingly rejected the Church's position on contraception.* One need only look at the dramatically falling rate of births within our faith to potentially conclude that not everyone is using the traditional natural family planning.

Since the Church will not allow this discussion to take place inside the life of the Church, clergy like myself who express such opinions may be suspended or removed from their assignments. The Church can punish the clergy, but they cannot punish the laity, who form their own values not only on the basis of the teachings of the Church, but also on their own morals and horse sense.

LOVE THY NEIGHBOR AS THYSELF

"Let each of you look not only to his own interests, but also to the interests of others."
—*Philippians 2:4*

Have you ever been around a group of high school boys, watching them cavort outside on the school grounds, or been in a car with them as they drive to the beach? If you have, then you probably noticed something that is essentially ever-present in their activities together. They tease each other a great deal.

Teasing by itself is not a bad thing. It depends on how it's done, to whom it's done, by whom it's done, and for what purpose it's done. Teasing in and of itself is not evil. However, teasing can indeed be evil, and it can be very, very destructive. If you pay close attention to teasing, you can tell on which side of the fence a particular incident falls.

Teasing could not be a universal attribute unless it's deeply tied into human nature. Although both men and women tease, I think that males have a much greater propensity to do so. Why they might do that is interesting, and I'll get to that shortly.

I made the statement that American males are more likely to be deeply involved with teasing than our girls. I can't prove that scientifically, but in terms of my own experience with lots of young people, to me it's almost universally true. I think that males, especially in their formative years as teenagers, are tremendously insecure. Teasing is a weapon that an insecure young boy can use against the other boys in the group in order to spotlight his greater powers, or more frequently, spotlight the weaknesses of one of the boys that he is playing with. At that point, it's still neither good nor bad.

I have a seat-of-the-pants rule about teasing that I've tried to live by, and that I've shared when I've given retreats or talks to young people. I call it "**the McCarthy Rule.**" I also share it with older people who are responsible for raising the next generation. They ought to be sensitive to the potential seriousness of teasing, and have a way to offer people the opportunity to tease without inflicting pain or real damage on the life of another person.

The McCarthy Rule is this: You can tease people all you want in areas where they are strong and confident.

If you tease people about their weaknesses, or about things which make them self-conscious, you run the risk of creating pain and destructiveness. Here is an example I use: The star athlete is almost down to the goal line, and he reaches back to catch the pass that is delivered to him perfectly, and he drops it. You can tease him about that. He's not going to enjoy the teasing, but he's a terrific athlete, and he can handle that. When the brightest girl or boy in class fails to get the highest grade on the test, you can tease them about that, because it's an area of their strength. Teasing can even be a motivation for working harder in that case.

But to tease people who are clumsy in their ability to be a really good ball player, or to tease people who are not overly endowed with academic ability about doing poorly, or being the slowest member of the class—*that's cruel and destructive.* If we can't be sure of someone's strengths, we'd probably be better off if we didn't tease at all.

Let me summarize. Teasing is a fact of life for most people. Some people get teased more, and some get teased less. If we're trying to live a good life, if we're trying to make life pleasant for the people around us, if we're trying to develop the best qualities in ourselves, then we need to be sensitive about the seriousness of teasing. This kind of sensitivity can help people be better. Teasing can be delightfully funny, but it also can be mean, petty, and destructive. If you're reading this book as a call to have a better attitude about life and to learn a lot of little things in the Christian tradition, then teasing is on the list.

If we find ourselves to be very sensitive, we need to be able to defend ourselves against teasing and be conscious of the fact that if the teasing is mean and hurtful, then the teaser is a weakling and using an unfair attack as a means to protect himself or herself. We should not always take teasing too personally. Many times the offender is simply unconscious of the harm that is being done.

Each of us needs to examine our conscience and see if there is any teasing in our lives that really hurts people. Do we generate laughs when a crowd is around at other people's expense? Do we make other people laugh by putting others on the verge of tears? An honest look might help you to be a better person.

THE ENTERTAINMENT MEDIA

- Bishop John's Pastoral Letter on the Entertainment Media

The performing arts have undergone unprecedented change and development in the last fifty years. Shakespeare or Bach could not have dreamed of the profusion of entertainment products we now create each year.

The values contained in television and other media products are supplanting church, community, and even family as primary determinants of cultural norms in our society. **We must ask ourselves: What values are being transmitted in these media products?**

In recent years, there has been a tragic collapse of standards of decency, morality, and honesty in television, movies, and popular music products. Disagreements among television and movie characters are now too often settled through violence. Intimate sexual relations are depicted as appropriate for the unmarried, and even the very young. Some forms of popular music encourage intolerance and promote violence, particularly toward women. Spiritual and religious dimensions of relationships are either ignored or trivialized.

Coincident with these trends, social changes of historic proportion have occurred. Since 1960, our society has experienced a dramatic decline in many "quality-of-life" indicators. The percentage of illegitimate births has soared from under 6 percent to over 26 percent, and divorce rates have quadrupled. The teen suicide rate increased by over 200 percent, and the violent crime rate by almost 400 percent. During this period, average daily television viewing increased almost 40 percent, while Scholastic Aptitude Test (SAT) scores dropped almost 80 points. Again, we must ask ourselves:

Is there a connection between this social downslide and the fall-off of standards in the media?

There is growing evidence of such a relationship. In recent years, social scientists have attributed the worsening societal statistics to an increase in self-indulgent and value-neutral behavior. Medical professionals have joined these scientists in asserting that the entertainment media, by glamorizing such behavior, contribute to this situation. These professionals point out that children, in particular, are formed and affected by the values of the broad community. When these values shatter—breaking down community and family stability—children are the first to suffer.

Some families, confronted with violent and sexually explicit programming, are turning off their televisions. Others are more closely monitoring the movies their children attend and the music they hear. Of course, many children without the benefit of involved parents continue to freely absorb the messages of these products.

I want to call on each of you to personally share in and encourage the positive changes underway in the entertainment media. Whether you are an artist, a business person, or solely a consumer, you can influence the quality of entertainment in our society. You can do this by adopting a Christ-centered standard of excellence.

If you are an artist or a businessperson in the entertainment industry, please examine your conscience when you create and offer your products. If you are a pastor, youth minister, or other parish leader, implement programs to educate the parish about quality criteria for entertainment products. To teach about media quality, consider using media education programs such as those offered through the Center for Media & Values. Also, encourage your youth to participate in the contests regularly carried in the entertainment section of *Catholic Spirit*. This is an excellent way to improve media literacy.

Let me also direct a special call to our youth. I know that the entertainment products of our culture have great attraction and appeal. But because these products have a power of personal formation, let me challenge you to accept Christ as your standard in their selection and use. You do not need to renounce art in order to follow Christ. In fact, Christ's church is a church of the artist, filled with the magnificent frescos of Michelangelo, the violent images of El Greco, and the music of Handel and Corelli. Art, through Christ, brings unique and revealing dimensions to life in this world.

I have defined a difficult mission for each of you today. Acting together, we can cause the entertainment media industry to serve its noble and legitimate purpose: to work in constructive service to society.

BULLYING

"I didn't have a father. So, in some ways, I was kind of a precocious kid...at any rate, that had the effect of making me a little bit different. I got along with the kids in my neighborhood, but I was an outsider when it came to the activities that they most enjoyed. I went to the Catholic Elementary School. We had to walk past a public school, and we were the "Catholickers," and we would get teased."
—Bishop John McCarthy

In an earlier segment, I referred to the issue of teasing. As an aspect of human interaction, teasing can have good qualities and be humorous, but if we're not careful, it can be harmful and destructive. Bullying behavior may overlap a great deal with teasing, but is distinctly different.

Bullying is a slang expression based on the fact that bulls in herds of cattle are usually the chiefs. They're the biggest, the strongest, and they usually get what they want. I think the word "bullying" originated from that fact because it almost always involves the physical ability to overpower (or at least to be perceived as capable of overpowering) another person.

Let me say this very clearly: teasing may have both good and bad aspects. *Bullying has only bad.* Teasing may flow from a person's ill-considered effort to be funny. Bullying flows from meanness, from pettiness, and most especially, it flows from cowardice! Bullies are cowards.

It's a regrettable aspect of human nature that young children quickly recognize differences between themselves. One may be more aggressive in their speech. Another has greater strength in their body, and more self-confidence in their athletic ability. Some are smarter, faster, or achieve more academically. Children become conscious at a young age of the diversity that separates them. Along with the consciousness of the diversity, a certain number of them recognize that they have certain strengths, real or imagined, that younger ones don't have. At that point, a human being can slip into the temptation to bully.

If the parents of these children act in a mindful way, guiding the children's recreation, supervising their classrooms, and leading these young people on outings, they can be attentive to those children who have a natural tendency to slide into the bad habit of bullying. Then a parent, coach, teacher, or older student can intervene at the moment the bullying begins, and redirect that young person into a more compassionate interaction.

One of the best ways to counteract bullying is to help the person who's tempted to bully understand that bullying is a reflection of cowardice, not strength. In reality, bullies are afraid they're inadequate, and they want to show that they don't have to be afraid because they are stronger. They can knock someone down faster than that person can knock them down. They can ridicule the other person and feel better about their own inadequacies.

This is where the differences between bullying and teasing become more obvious. Mean-spirited teasing is very often the most common form of bullying. There are many students who dread going to school or getting on the bus in the morning or afternoon because they know they are going to face a tremendous amount of bullying. Sometimes they're hit, but mostly they are ridiculed. Whether they're redheaded, have braces, or are too fat or skinny, too short or too tall, they are in some way different from the crowd.

Bullying is almost always a form of cowardice. The label of "coward" is one of the worst things we can call a person, regardless of age. If that weapon is used against the bully, it can have real and lasting results. It doesn't universally work, because the person who is doing the bullying may not be physically or psychologically afraid of the person being abused. The bully is afraid, however, of his own inadequacy. She or he is going to build her- or himself up by tearing somebody else down. This person is not only a coward, but is also destructive. If you explain to a young person that bullying is a form of cowardice, this has a tremendous impact. Telling them they are destructive simply doesn't carry the same punch, because they really can't visualize the long-term damage being done when we upset a human being's process of formation, growth, or maturing.

When we talk about teasing, we need to distinguish whether it's gentle humor spotlighting the talents of the person being teased, or whether it's an effort to hurt somebody and draw pleasure out of inflicting pain upon another. Teasing can go either way, but bullying cannot. Bullying is always wrong. It's a reflection of cowardice and long-term destructiveness. You may have trouble reaching a thirteen-year-old boy who has a tendency toward bullying, but we need to try. You must give him or her the clear message that bullying doesn't pay off—in the home, in the classroom, or on the street. *The bully needs to be disciplined—immediately, and with appropriate clarity and intensity, in order to change this cruel behavior before it becomes a life-long habit.*

Let me make one additional point here. In the world of religious practice, of religious discussion and faith, some people are capable of an extraordinarily destructive form of bullying—***religious bullying***. Inside the Catholic Church, this was not too common before the second Vatican Council, because the vast majority of us felt like we understood the Apostle's Creed and the Ten Commandments, and lived by it. However, after Vatican II, there was a certain relaxation in particular areas of religious practice, and ultimately, for some people, in religious values.

There are one billion, two hundred million Roman Catholics in the world, and they are often divided—too simplistically in my opinion—into liberals and conservatives. The liberals in general do not bully the conservatives, perhaps because they don't care what the conservatives think. Basically, the liberals ignore the conservatives. The conservatives, however, care mightily, and will stand firm and fight for their convictions.

In some contentious settings, if a priest makes a mistake in his sermon one week, he's likely to find that the next Sunday there are a half—dozen members of the congregation holding tape recorders. On Monday morning, those people will all be at the Chancery office to file a complaint, standing in the position of "I do not agree with you, and therefore I'm going to correct you." This attitude causes a lot of pain, and is absolutely a form of bullying. It needs to stop, whether it occurs within our Church, or out in the workplace or playground.

Obviously, there is also religious bullying not only between various Christian denominations, but also between Christian and non-Christian faiths. Again, let me be clear, this type of behavior is never acceptable. We certainly can disagree and even debate our different points of view, but none of us have a directive from God that tells us to force others how to worship and behave.

If we stress the destructiveness of bullying with our children and young people, it could be lessened in our society. I believe that it's a disease that naturally expands, and I think that some of our wars may even be an international expression of this disease.

HEALTHCARE

"I was the only Catholic Bishop publicly supporting the Affordable Healthcare Act."
—Bishop John McCarthy

You never can predict the outcome of answering the telephone (unless, of course, you have caller ID.) The other day I picked up the phone, and it was the Associated Press, inquiring about my views on the health care reform bill before the House and Senate. Naturally, I told them that while it was imperfect, it would be a tremendous step forward in moving our society towards a more just health system.

The next day in the morning paper, I discovered *I was the ONLY Catholic Bishop in the country publicly taking that position.* Perhaps I'm not too lonely, though, because the nuns joined me—or, more correctly, I joined them. That's why the decision was easy for me. After attending a great Catholic school in the 1930s, I learned to always do what the sisters say! All kidding aside, though, I am happy to be in full agreement with the leadership of the Catholic religious women, as we both feel the far greater good of this health care bill outweighed any merely potential detriments.

Good health is one of the greatest gifts a person can possibly have, but with the nature of life on this planet, there are endless threats against good health. We're lucky that in the last two centuries, the world of medicine has made awesome strides in countering disease and various forms of serious health risks such as accidents. While we now have an awesome array of information and competence in dealing with health problems, until recently we have not developed a system to make them available to everyone in the country. I believe this situation is worsened by the almost complete dependence on the fee-for-service system. Not that doctors shouldn't be paid—of course they should, and paid fully in accordance with their skills and education. But the United States is the only developed nation on the planet that still uses this method of providing health care.

What if the fire department refused to come and put out the fire raging through your house because you owed them money? Shouldn't basic health care operate under the same concept—that everyone in the United States has a right to a certain level of care? Starting with Teddy Roosevelt, through FDR, Truman, Nixon, and Clinton, presidents over the last century have seen the inadequacy of the system and have sought to improve it. They all failed.

When Barack Obama was running for the presidency, he made health care reform his number-one domestic issue. He was new. He was young, and he was Black. Many people did not take him seriously. The fact is, however, that in March of 2010, the Congress of the United States, following the leadership of the President, has now enacted landmark legislation that will cover 95% of this nation's population. It's a complex measure with rough edges, but the fact is that the United States of America has said that each and every one of its citizens has a right to health care, and that it will now be provided.

Was there controversy involved in bringing this plan to fruition? You bet your boots there was! Even the Catholic Bishops—*although they have been pushing health care reform for over ninety years (since 1919)*—stood in opposition to the President's bill in what they feared was going to be its final form. The Bishops feared that a policy would come through the back door that would fund abortions with public money, even though *the bill expressly forbade it.* I thought the Bishops were using poor judgment, since they were running the risk of losing the entire program by applying the old cliché, "**the search for the perfect often destroys the good.**"

NARCISSISM

"You will be like God," says the snake.

—Genesis 3:5

You'd be hard pressed to find an older adult Roman Catholic who did not know about the Church's teaching on a sad subject called Original Sin. We've heard it all our lives, and frequently when someone we know does a very bad thing or we ourselves do something evil, we tend to half-humorously write it off with a quip such as "What do you expect? It's original sin!"

Of course, we do think that original sin is behind all of human weakness, and that it is a continuing form of suffering that sadly distorts our natural drive toward being happy, well-balanced people. So when we're faced with embezzlement, adultery, vicious personal cruelty, and a host of other weaknesses, we tend to give ourselves a free ride by merely referencing original sin. We say, "Yes, this was bad, but it's really Adam and Eve's fault—we can't really be blamed." While our faith teaches the objective truth of original sin, the Church has never used it as an explanation for or justification of freely chosen actions or decisions. WE are responsible for ourselves.

Someone might ask, "How does original sin manifest itself in our daily lives?" Well, frankly, it does not appear under the headings of the major evil actions mentioned above, but is more frequently present throughout the day and throughout our lives under the heading of narcissism. Narcissism is pervasive in the human condition. There are few if any of us who are not touched by its damaging effects. The range of narcissism, however, is almost as wide as the human personality. In some people, it's barely detectable, and because of excellent self-control, may never be known by those who are observing our actions, and more importantly, speculating about our motivations. In others, however, narcissism can move out to the front edge of our lives and be so pervasive that it is destructive of our relationship with others, and ultimately—and this is the divine boomerang—destructive of ourselves as well.

Narcissism is a negative quality which causes us to see everything that is occurring in terms of our own personal desires and needs, regardless of the negative implications that those desires and needs inflict in the lives of those around us. We see our innate situation and environment in terms of our personal benefit, our needs, and our desires. This naturally has serious, painful ramifications for those around us.

There is an element of objective truth in the basic narcissist tendency. When a person is standing in front of a large audience, the audience is indeed in front of him or her, the electricians working behind the scenes are really behind him, and people moving up or down the aisle are on the speaker's right or left. In a very concrete sense, it is not a problem that we see ourselves as the center of our physical world. However, we should not let that perception extend beyond the physical! We do not have the right or freedom to judge every other aspect of our lives as though we were the center of it.

Now, sometimes the situation heals itself. When you walk into the room of a sick friend, you are hopefully aware of that person's vulnerability and need for assistance, information, or encouragement. This type of circumstance happily overwhelms narcissistic tendencies. But if instead, when we hear a sad story of trouble and difficulty, and we find ourselves waiting for that person to pause in their litany of woes and take a breath so that we can tell that person what real trouble is from our point of view, that's narcissism.

We all know that there are ten basic commandments, and that those ten primitive enactments of divine law can be amplified to cover every imaginable human failure or sin. The fact is that most humans sin, and most if not all sins are reducible to narcissism. The Christian tradition has held that the basic sin of Adam and Eve is not the sin of rebellion, but the sin of *pride*. But even in the simple words of Genesis, you can see the truth when beautiful Eve, sans garments, hears the enticing words of the snake: "Eat this, and you will be like God, knowing good from evil." That is pride, it is rebellion, and in terms of modern terminology, it's narcissism.

The vast majority of sexual sins occur because of the thought, "I want to enjoy this violation of the 6th commandment (adultery) because I think it will make ME happy." And then there's theft: we steal because we decide, "I need this." When we're tempted to steal the car, it's because we think WE can use it and the price is right. When we malign our neighbor's good reputation, it's because WE think it is pleasurable to pull them down and simultaneously elevate ourselves because of their diminution.

What should we do about this pervasive, almost universal weakness? I have a couple of concrete suggestions. One is to say over and over to ourselves, in our prayers, in our sleep, and while we're fighting through urban traffic, "I am not the center of the world! I am not the center of the world!" If we say that often enough, we will actually start to believe it, and we will cut back on the narcissistic tendencies in our lives. The next thing I would suggest is a systematic effort to develop the awesome, creative virtue of empathy, which is the other side of recognizing that we are not the center of the world. Empathy is the natural virtue that with effort can be developed to a high degree that enables us to instinctively and quickly put ourselves into the other person's position. The Native Americans have a wonderful saying: "One should not judge another until he has walked in his moccasins." This is an excellent illustration of the need for empathy.

Strictly speaking, narcissism exists in the life of an individual, but when enough individuals share the weakness of narcissism, it's possible that narcissistic tendencies will manifest not just in the one human person, but can be translated into the structures and organizations that people build when working together. This could be true of a medical association, or a national government. I must say that even churches are not exempt from this either. All in all, narcissism and its implications are a sad element of the human condition. The good news is that we are free beings, and we can overcome its strong pull as individuals, as organizations, and as a society. To the extent that we are able to do this, our quality of life and our degree of happiness will be greatly enhanced.

THE IMPORTANCE OF VALUES

*"I think the lack of religious values in our society is
what's making us the very sick and confused society that we are."*
—Bishop John McCarthy, in an interview in the Austin Chronicle

Recently, I was watching the evening news on television, and there was a story about a small group of primitive people living deep in the depths of the Brazilian jungle. Their habitat was so removed from the modern world that it was virtually untouched. In portraying their lives, the camera documented in a very dramatic way how these people lived life from day to day. The children were joyous, the parents were loving, and the village was protective of its communal life.

Regretfully, however, the storyline was not about the wonderful nature of their simple life, but rather the fear and terror that gripped them as they felt that the world they knew, loved, and enjoyed was soon going to be taken away from them.

Should they have been elated over the possibility that they would soon benefit from modern medicine? Should they have been cheered up by the fact that in a few years, the Brazilian government would bring schools? Should they have felt more secure knowing that their terribly difficult jungle environment would soon experience paved roads? Not at all. What they realized was that their world, as they knew it, was about to be disrupted and destroyed.

These people had a culture that they knew, that they understood, with which they were comfortable, and which they loved. The idea of having it all taken away from them was indeed a frightening and horrible fate to consider.

The men taught the boys how to use the bow and arrow and to catch fish in the stream with a spear. The girls learned what was necessary in order to keep their dwellings in the village properly supplied and cared for. This was their life, and they knew and loved it.

This scenario, in my opinion, documents the importance of culture and community and values in order for individuals or people to have a satisfying and fulfilling life. It has very little to do with wealth in the modern sense. What makes life worth living is the value system with which we live. These simple people in the heart of Brazil knew what they had, and they were happy.

The Economist is one of the most prominent magazines in the world, and a few issues back, the lead story focused on the "unhappy Americans." The story described the startling contrast between the wealth and prosperity of the United States and the incidence of alcoholism, drug addiction, sexual deviation, divorce, violence, emotionally disturbed children, and drug use. *The Economist* merely reported on the facts; they did not offer a solution.

The great religious family (which is the Church) does offer a solution—or more accurately, the proper medicine—but like castor oil, not everyone races to grab it. The Church endeavors to teach us that there is a value system out there based upon our nature. In our faith, that system comes ultimately from God Himself. This value system is encoded in a simple form in what we call the Ten Commandments. Isn't it interesting that there are millions of civil laws—at least three thousand laws in the Catholic Church—and God got by with just ten, and two overlap?

The Ten Commandments govern the three basic relationships in our life: first of all, the relationship we have with God; secondly, our relationship with those with whom we share life; and finally, the relationship we have with ourselves. When we live the generous, realistic life encoded in the Commandments, we're not going to be free of pain. Cavities can still hurt. Our brother-in-law may still divorce our sister. But there will be a calm understanding of who we are, where we are, and how we ought to live.

Our Brazilian brothers and sisters deep in the heart of the Amazon know how to live by their values, and for them, that was the secret of a successful life. Let me make a harsh statement about modern American life.

The people of the United States have not yet devised a method of transferring values in a way that has universal applicability.

Are there not millions of Americans, Jews, Christians, Muslims, and others who successfully transfer their values to their children? Absolutely, and for that we can thank God. But the United States as a nation has not developed a true system of teaching and passing on our moral values. We all know about the separation of Church and State, and thank God and our Founding Fathers for it. It is possibly the best gift they left us. *However, separation of church and state has been erroneously interpreted over the last fifty or sixty years to mean that the voice and force of religion is to be totally excluded from the public life of the country.*

How are we prepared to live our lives as responsible citizens? For the majority of us, our public school system is a very important aspect of life, and yet that same majority is denied any type of formation in morals and the mystery and purpose of life and how we ought to relate to each other. The public policy of this country is that life's purpose cannot be known or taught, and if someone has a view on that, the parents are perfectly free to transfer that value system to their children. That's wonderful—it means there is still an element of freedom in the country. However, can you imagine a high school principal standing in front of the class and saying that this year, they will learn their math at home, and their parents will be responsible for teaching this subject? By the way, we will tie you up eight hours a day, Monday through Friday, so if they want to teach that math, they'll have to do it Saturday morning, and you won't be able to play on the soccer team.

I'm proud of the great work that families and churches are doing to try to fill this void in the lives of their children and their neighborhood. However, it puts the kids going to religious education classes at an awkward time, which results in an unhappy attitude on the part of many of the young people. Studying their faith is often a pain in the neck.

About fifty or sixty years ago, when the country began to realize that it was creating an obstacle to the transfer of values, a number of innovative attempts were made by public educators and church leaders to develop a program that would enable religious values to be transferred in a way that did not do violence to the constitutional demand for the separation of church and state, and at the same time, would give the religious forces in our society greater access to the children that they have a natural right to reach.

The first effort was to release the public school teachers at a certain time each week, and then churches would send in qualified teachers to give religious instruction. There were logistical problems and complications, of course. Students had to move around to get in the class of their family's choosing, so the Methodists would get Methodist teachings, and Catholics get Catholic teaching, etc. Atheists took exception to the concept, and sued until it was declared unconstitutional.

The next effort was to release the children to leave the school early to go to a nearby church for instruction. That, too, was declared unconstitutional. Personally, I don't think today's Supreme Court would come down with the same ruling. Precedents are very powerful in the judicial system, and therefore those prohibitions are very much in place today.

The Brazilian natives are terrified of losing their rights, their power to transfer their values to their children. In the United States, we virtually gave up that right fifty years ago.

Thoughtful people should begin to think and pray over whether or not we want to grow old as part of the only culture on the planet that does not seem to believe in the importance of handing down its moral and religious values.

THE PRODIGAL SON

*"The lost sheep and the prodigal son are not merely colorful figures
used by our Lord in His preaching. Today they are living
among us as real and concrete human beings."*
—Bishop John McCarthy, in a Pastoral Letter on Sacraments

One of the reasons that Jesus Christ is the second person of the Blessed
Trinity, that He dwelt among us as one with us, is because God wanted
the human family to grasp the reality of His love for us on a level that
we could understand. When you think about love, you think about men
loving beautiful women, parents loving wonderful children, and families
coming together for reunions and anniversaries where everyone is in a good
mood. That kind of love is easy and natural, but it's not the only time when
love should manifest itself.

It's sometimes challenging to love in difficult situations—to love your
son when he has been booked for the second time on cocaine possession; to
love your daughter-in-law when, without any obvious reason, she has left
your son and their three children; to love somebody when they've embez-
zled funds from your husband's business, and should be going to jail but
somehow slipped through the system and is off scot-free. When you're up
against that kind of meanness, that lack of kindness, then love is very, very
difficult. Those are the kinds of realities that caused Jesus to talk to the
apostles about love. He did it a number of times, but one of his most wonderful parables is the story of the prodigal son.

Everybody knows the story of the prodigal son. Prodigal means irre-
sponsible, selfish, and wasteful. Everyone can identify with the story. The

kid is a jerk! The kid is ungrateful. He's immoral, selfish, and thinks only of himself and his own gratification. He dissipates what his father's hard work has put together over the years. But finally, the son begins to realize what he's done, and he comes home.

It's a great story. The old man is watching for him. In his flat country, he can see a long way off. He sees a cloud of dust, and sees it's someone coming towards him. He wonders if it could possibly be his long-lost son. He hopes and prays, and then runs out towards him, and realizes it is his son. The son is wearing rags, he's underweight and dirty, and he's very, very humble. He falls on his knees and begs his father to forgive him. The forgiveness had already occurred. The father was there, waiting for him, reaching for him because he loved him. He loved him in the face of the dirt, the immorality, the selfishness, and all those weak aspects of human nature. The son happily accepts his love and forgiveness. Symbolically, the father calls for a celebration. "Kill the fatted calf. Take those rags off him and put a rich robe on his shoulders. Get him cleaned up, and we're going to have a great party." Everybody knows that.

However, an important part of the story of the prodigal son is the tail end, when the self-righteous brother comes home. He's never done any bad things. He points out that he's never done any of those things. He was always there, always working. He was faithful. Now, he's very jealous and very unhappy that there's a party going on for his useless brother. His father comes to him and asks, "What's wrong? Aren't you happy that your brother is back?" The brother lets him know he is not, because he's not receiving that kind of honor. The father says, "Look, I've always loved you, and you've always been here. We're celebrating because your brother was dead, now he's alive." In our terms now, we'd say it was the resurrection of the brother.

The text doesn't give us any indication of whether or not the second son ever came into the house. I'd bet he left. The sad thing is that the older brother becomes the prodigal son. What's being exchanged in the story is love. The failed love initially by the prodigal son is compensated for by his humble return and admission of his own weakness, and the acceptance of his father's love. The father loved both his sons, but his love manifested differently because the circumstances of the two were so different. There is no love shown from the second son—either for the brother, or for the father.

And therein lies the real story of the prodigal son: it's the other brother who is the real prodigal son.

So what should we learn from this story? We should learn the importance of forgiveness. This man sought his father's forgiveness, but he also seems to have had the capability to forgive himself. He accepts the gifts from his father, and is heading in to enjoy the banquet. We should have that same calm confidence in God's forgiveness. He forgives us everything! *There is destructiveness in the failure to forgive.* In the absence of forgiveness, there may be hatred and bitterness, and this creates spiritual disease that really eats at a person's being.

Parables are open-ended. The reason that they are still here after two thousand years is that they are open to many different interpretations and possibilities. There are only one or two places where Jesus is specific about what each word means. In general, each parable has one overriding point. Everything else is just a mosaic to get to that point. I believe the point of this parable is that God's love is so awesome that we don't deserve it, we don't produce it, and we haven't earned it.

Once we have grasped the reality of being loved infinitely, earthly rewards are less important.

AN INTERVIEW WITH BISHOP JOHN MCCARTHY

Bishop John, what are you most proud of accomplishing in your years as a priest?

Proud? I'm not sure about that, but I guess the thing that *pleases* me the most is that I found myself for more than half a century deeply involved in the lives of thousands of families, in those areas of their lives that are most meaningful and frequently painful—and I pray that I was good influence. I was there for births, for deaths, in the aftermath of domestic violence, for graduations, for surgeries, for hope and despair. And, please God, mostly I was there for faith! Countless baptisms, confirmations, reconciliations—and let's not leave out the Eucharist. What I am essentially saying is that in doing my job, I could be proud of carrying out the work of Jesus of Nazareth.

What did you enjoy most about being a bishop?

There is no doubt about this: what I enjoyed most is that the Church has structured the office of bishop in such a way that it can *really solve problems*—it can truly resolve conflict and generate peace and harmony.

How can a bishop solve problems?

The bishop has extraordinary practical powers over personnel, finances, general direction, and missionary thrust—every aspect of the life of the

Church. The sad part is that much of that power is not used effectively by many bishops. Someone comes in with a new idea—a vision of improvement—but visions involve risk. It's easier to say, "No, we simply don't do it that way. We never did it before, and we are not going to start now." Vision involves risk. *There is typically no risk in saying no.* Bureaucrats are against vision, because change is so threatening. I chose to embrace change.

Concretely, what did you accomplish?

I think I brought to my ministry a more unified vision or concept of how parish life is to be structured. When I entered the seminary, all parishes had churches and schools. They were committed to education and liturgy. I felt something was missing.

The role of the parish is to make real and concrete in *this* place, at *this* time, what Jesus did. Jesus taught; we have schools and religious education. Jesus worshipped; every parish centers its life on prayer and worship. *But Jesus also lessened pain!* The most visible parts of His ministry, along with teaching and ministering, were his miracles and his acts: curing the blind, feeding the hungry, protecting oppressed people, and so forth. In this context, I began to talk, to write, and to carry out the restructuring first of my parish, and then subsequently, of the dioceses in which I served. My goal was to raise this third component of the life of Jesus to be on an equal footing with those other two, which had always been present. I called it *social ministry.*

How did you implement your new "social ministry"?

The first step in implementing a social ministry was to find the right person to be the director of this vital service—either full time or volunteer. A budget was provided, as well as a format for what ministry was needed and should be carried out in this parish at this time. Of course, whether a parish is large or small, affluent or poor, the level of pain is always high and present. Alcoholism, drug abuse, domestic violence, unemployment, emotional disorders, etc., are always there. Each of these simple words involve a great deal of human pain and suffering, and the Church can give real meaning and assistance to those people still suffering if it structures itself in a way to respond effectively to these needs.

The pastor should know his parish, and therefore, know which needs are most pressing. Additionally, the pastor should be able to motivate large numbers of parishioners to become directly involved. Dozens, if not hundreds, of volunteers, must back up the social ministry director. No one person has to do everything! Some people may want to help by simply driving elderly people to their doctors or the grocery store.

On a different level, a credit union, for example (properly run, I must add), can be a real tool for self-improvement in a poverty-stricken area. In both churches where I was in charge, new credit unions helped make a difference. In this financial arena, however, I would offer great caution: to be successful, credit unions must be sizable.

What were some of the greatest social ministry needs that you were able to address?

When I mentioned the power and resources available to the diocesan bishop, I noted that through these, a bishop has the opportunity to do good things. I'm not going to give you a laundry list of my activities in those twenty-five years during which I exercised the office of bishop, but I would like to mention two unique organizations that are extremely important to me.

One is what I simply call "**the Law Project.**" I was able to draw into a loose organization approximately 120 lawyers who were willing to do pro-bono work in Austin on the average of about four hours every two months. In cooperation with the city of Austin, we ran two law clinics per week in different parts of the city. With no publicity or advertising whatsoever, when we opened the doors at 6pm, there would be thirty to forty people who considered themselves to be in frightening trouble. The primary gift that we were able to present was first-rate legal advice when it was sorely needed. This is a gift that is frequently beyond the reach of the poor, and causes them to get in much greater trouble than they would with good advice. I've been out of office for twelve years, but many of these lawyers have continued this work even today.

Saint Louise House is the quite simply the most meaningful social effort with which I have ever been involved, and of which I am sinfully proud. Simply stated, Saint Louise House is a program brought together by a handful of St. Austin's parishioners to provide housing for home-less women with children. When they first came to me with this idea, I flat-out told them it couldn't be done. I warned them about the liability and costs that would be involved. I mentioned the familial dangers that could develop. Despite my words of "wisdom", they purchased a twelve-unit apartment complex for $650,000. Since then, they have expanded to forty-eight units. Saint Louise House set up apartments, fully stocking them so that when the family moves in, they have everything from pots and pans to furniture, and when they leave, they carry forward this entire set of household provisions for their next apartment. I am delighted to share that I was dead wrong, and Saint. Louise House is a thriving, vibrant social ministry dramatically and permanently changing the lives of women and their children.

What other changes did you encourage or create?

I grew up in the diocese of Galveston and Houston, with over 125 parishes—most of them sizable. When I became a pastor, I found myself the only full-time priest serving about 1,200 families—a fairly sizable job, if you take it seriously! As I found myself ordering toilet tissue for the boy's bathroom and making arrangements to have those two broken win-dows replaced, I asked myself—is this the best use of my priestly time? Or should I secure the services of a more competent person, and stick to liturgy, preaching, and social ministry?

Fifty years later, all sizable parishes have impressive lay-staffs, which is why we are able to continue to stumble forward with an inadequate number of priests. This may seem like an obvious change, but at the time I first suggested delegating to others the non-priest-required but essential church housekeeping tasks, it was a novel concept. God bless the lay staffs in the parishes across the United States!

What was different for you when you reached the Diocesan level?

At the diocese, I came to a deeper understanding of the totality of church ministry. I moved beyond parish social service, and came to grips with what the Church has always known was an essential component of its makeup: a missionary thrust. The last words of Jesus were His commissioning of the apostles to become missionaries to Jerusalem, Judea and Samaria… and to the ends of the earth. By 1980, I had realized that Texas was indeed, one of those "ends of the earth."

I urged parishes to set up within their structure not only finance and education committees, but also a missionary committee. I still firmly believe that no parish council should hold a meeting without asking itself, "What did we do last month, and how successful was it in terms of the missionary thrust of our parish?"

Pulling parish missionary groups together, I established the Diocesan Mission Council, and from there it was a natural step to the annual Texas Mission Conference. I was happy and proud that most of the dioceses joined in that common effort. When we say mission, or missionary thrust, we are dealing with any action, organization, or structure that makes Jesus of Nazareth better known, loved, and served. It can be helping with a diocesan newspaper, gathering used clothing for poor villages in Mexico, raising funds for famine in Ethiopia, or helping to support two Dominican sisters working in Guatemala. The very essence of the Church is missionary.

Bishop John, you are well known for reaching out to other non-Catholic Christian leaders (as well as other faiths). What have you done differently than other Catholic leaders?

I grew up in the 1930's with an Irish mother who was totally committed to Catholicism, and she never saw any blemishes or weaknesses in the wonderful Church that she loved so much. I shared that view myself, until my work led me into the reality where I could perceive that yes, the Church presents the message of Jesus, but that message is presented through very human structures. *As such, those structures can be, on occasion, inadequate or incompetent.*

I learned that there were very real and justifiable causes for the Reformation in the 16th Century, and I realized that my Protestant brothers and sisters had deep faith and generous concern for the well being of the world in which they found themselves. This led me, at the parish level, to reach out to my neighboring pastors, and in the process I enjoyed wonderful experiences with men and women who shared my faith but not my ecclesiology.

As a Bishop, I automatically served on the board of the Texas Conference of Churches. This conference was born immediately after the second Vatican council, when Roman Catholics finally decided they could attend and be part of Protestant Church services and organizations with only a limited chance of going to Hell. The Texas Conference of Churches (TCC) was a wonderful dream, and the dream is still alive, but activating it has proven to be difficult. In the early '90's, I aggressively attempted to resurrect the conference and give it new vitality. I was moderately successful, but I regret to say that today it is but a shadow of what it ought to be.

What are your feelings about "relaxing the rules" of the Catholic Church?

I have a very strong view about the personality that Jesus of Nazareth presents to us through the gospel narratives, which is that He always combined strength and gentleness. He faced his enemies with courage. But he dealt with those who were suffering with generosity and concern. I also believe that the essential mission of the Church is to make Jesus present in a given time and place. Therefore, the Church should blend strength and gentleness.

One of the sad things about church leaders is that they are very enthusiastic about the strength, and less so about the gentleness. It's so easy to be oblivious to human suffering if you are not immersed in it. It's simple to avoid additional work by simply telling people, "No, you can't do that." Large and complex organizations involving millions of members have to have goals, policies, and rules, but they should never be applied with blind and insensitive rigor.

This applies in a very special way to the everyday life of the parish. For example, when a couple wants to make arrangements for a wedding, they should be embraced with joy and love—not handed a 13-page memo on how we do that at St. Matthews (there is time for that later on). When a proud young couple comes forward to baptize their child, they should again be received with thanks, encouragement, and joy. Whether or not they are properly registered with the parish should not be the FIRST thing to be discussed, and if there is a problem regarding the sacrament of matrimony (has there been a prior divorce?), that can be handled later.

In my years as a bishop, I found myself continuing to try to convince the priests and deacons—and sadly enough, often the church secretaries—to deal with people in a way that reflects that they understand that these people are reaching out to Jesus of Nazareth. It's tragic that they are frequently treated by a response that is more in keeping with General Motors Corporation. Rules are important, but they are man-made, and should be administered with the love of Jesus.

PHOTOGRAPHS

Grace O'Brien McCarthy with her boys,
Frank, John and Joe, circa 1938

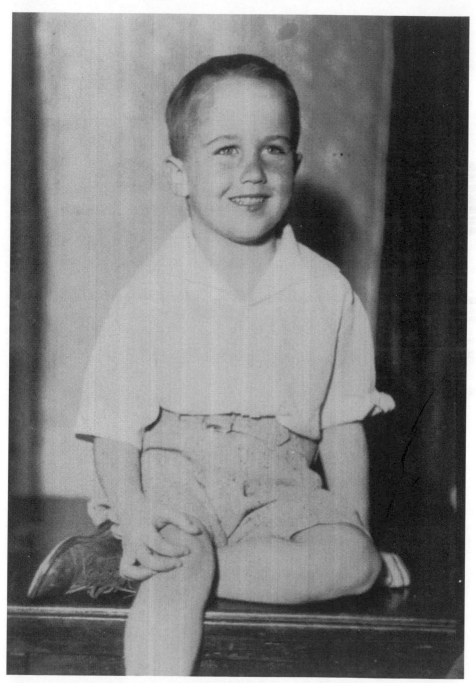

JOHN, 5, GREW UP AT 224 CORTLANDT ST. IN THE HOUSTON HEIGHTS

ALL SAINTS SCHOOL, HOUSTON, 1941
—JOHN IS IN 2ND BOTTOM ROW, 4TH FROM RIGHT

MAY 1956 AT ORDINATION IN GALVESTON

1963: St. Cecelia Church in West Houston, Assistant Pastor McCarthy's going-away party

No one else caught fish that day in Mexico...

On the street in Mexico City, a handheld
bell draws >1,000 people to Mass, 1966

Fr. John taking a siesta in Mexico

JOHN JOKINGLY STRUGGLES TO CONTROL HIS MODEST YOUTHFUL
ASPIRATIONS: ST. PETERS IN ROME, 1966

PRAYING FOR A SPIRITUAL REVIVAL IN SAN PAULO, BRAZIL, 1972

ORDINATION AS AUXILIARY BISHOP OF GALVESTON & HOUSTON, AT ST. THERESA'S, HOUSTON, 1978, PHOTO BY JACK PURYEAR

Staff Photo by Larry Kolvoord

Archbishop John McCarthy: 'People will see that I'm an open and available person.'

Bishop installed in Austin Diocese

By Joe Vargo
American-Statesman Staff

The Rev. John Edward McCarthy was installed as the third bishop of the Austin Diocese Wednesday, accepting the position of religious leader of Central Texas' 200,000 Roman Catholics with "faith, joy and enthusiasm."

McCarthy, 55, who came to Austin from the Diocese of Galveston-Houston where he served as auxiliary bishop since 1979, also pledged his commitment to "the well-being" of society as a whole.

"To men and women of goodwill in Austin, Travis County and Central Texas, you will find in me a solid willingness to work together for justice," McCarthy told a crowd of more than 6,000 who came to the Erwin Center. "That's a promise."

The crowd included about 500 priests and nuns from Texas and 34 bishops and archbishops from throughout the United States. There were also rabbis from at least two Austin synagogues and bishops from the Lutheran and Episcopal churches.

McCarthy was installed by Archbishop Patrick Flores of San Antonio, a close friend who was ordained with McCarthy in 1956. Flores called McCarthy a "zealous priest, an understanding

BISHOP JOHN INSTALLED AS DIOCESAN BISHOP
REPRINTED WITH PERMISSION OF THE
AUSTIN-AMERICAN STATESMAN, 1984

WITH DR. PAT HAYES, PRESIDENT OF ST. EDWARDS UNIVERSITY.
(BISHOP JOHN IS LOYAL SUPPORTER OF ST. EDWARDS UNIVERSITY)

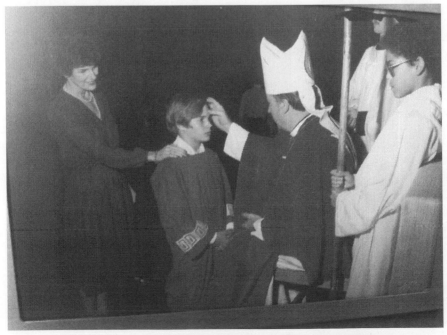

CELEBRATING THE SACRAMENT OF CONFIRMATION

Irish Humor: The Bookcase

I was profoundly moved by the funeral of Pope Paul VI, which was in 1978. The funeral took place in the Piazza, in front of St. Peter's. Behind St. Peter's was this enormous façade of the world's largest church. And beside it are hundreds of thousands of people jammed into the area, and bishops in robes and everything, and yet they had his body in a pine box on the ground with six simple candles on either side of him.

I thought that was so meaningful- with all that wealth and power and ostentation, this is the reality of death: a pine box. We just have to get rid of this extra stuff here, this body.

Personally, I already have my coffin. And I use it as a bookshelf. It sits there open in my home. The top is nailed to the back- it's the old traditional coffin. All the books in this case are about Ireland. The Irish, who suffered terribly from oppression for 700 years, jokingly say that death is a solution, not a problem. I love that! We confront death, and when it occurs we have big celebrations. Let me be clear, we are not celebrating death itself. We are simply celebrating that this death is the opening of a door into eternity.

—Bishop John McCarthy

A BISHOP AMONG BISHOPS: ALL SAINTS DAY MASS, ST. THERESA'S
CATHOLIC SCHOOL, AUSTIN, TEXAS

RETIREMENT MASS FOR THESE TWO IRISHMEN, MSGR.
MARK DEERING, IN WACO, 2000.

"A PRIEST, A RABBI AND A MINISTER ARE PLAYING GOLF..."
ALWAYS READY FOR A GOOD JOKE!

"Retired" as the Bishop, but still full time Roman Catholic
priest, educator, & servant

BISHOP JOHN SHARING A LAUGH WITH FRIEND & EDITOR, JILL GRIMES

Traditions and Practices

"This is one of the great strengths of Catholicism—signs and symbols. We love them! Some of them are insignificant, unimportant. But some of them we believe are the very essence of the inner life of the church."

"For instance, when you go inside the church, you remember that 'the inner life of the Church is built around signs that Jesus is still with us.' That is the essential component of what we call the Sacraments: that Jesus, for us, is not just a historical figure in books with Julius Caesar, Napoleon, and Franklin D. Roosevelt. Jesus was real, and He *is* real."

"So, without going through all the theology, we believe that the followers of Jesus are in some mysterious sense united with their Savior, Jesus of Nazareth. We believe that that union begins, the first time, when we are baptized. So then, when you come to the Eucharist, the essence of the church—regardless of whether we use the term from the scholastic period of philosophy, trans-substantiation—is that in some way, that Jewish carpenter who lived in what we call the Holy Land 2000 years ago is still mysteriously present. And this sign that we use—bread and wine—is the sign of his presence. And we believe it is very real."

—Bishop John McCarthy

THE BIBLE

*"In the Catholic Church, the Bible does not come first; it comes out of
the Magisterium, which is the unbroken tradition of the Church."*
—Bishop John McCarthy

Is the Bible a Catholic book? For the vast majority of the people of the United
States, the Bible is a factor in their lives in many different ways. This is espe-
cially true for people of the mainline Protestant faith groups, e.g., Methodists,
Presbyterians, Baptists, Lutherans, etc. The Catholic Church's membership
is nearly twice the size of all the Protestant churches currently present in the
United States. A very valid question would be, "Is the Holy Bible, which
Christians almost universally revere as God's word, as important to the Roman
Catholic as it is to their brothers and sisters in the Protestant faith groups?"

The theoretical answer is that it certainly is, but a more practical reply
would be that it is not. Prior to the second Vatican council, the average
Catholic received very little formal study in sacred scripture. Theology, of
course, would be a powerful force in the education of Catholics. Deference
would be paid to the importance of the Bible, but in terms of classes, study,
week-to-week use, its absence was rather obvious.

The second council has made a determined effort to turn this unhappy
situation around and motivate Catholics to appreciate the Bible and make
ever-greater use of it, both in their religious formation and in their worship, as well as in their liturgical ceremonies.

Why was the Bible underutilized in the Roman Catholic Church until
the 1960s?

Part of the answer is that while Catholics love and revere the sacred
texts of the Bible, they look at it quite differently than other Christian

communities. For Protestants, the Bible provides the basis for their faith and their reason for existence. "Nothing but the Bible" is the underlying principle as enunciated by Martin Luther with his famous statement "sola scriptura" (the Bible alone).

Let me restrict myself for a few moments to the New Testament. Catholics do not believe that the New Testament is the foundation for the Church. We hold that the Church itself is the foundation for the Church. Rather than the Church coming out of the New Testament, the historical fact is that the New Testament comes out of the Church.

In the second and third centuries, there were many, many writings about Jesus, His teachings, and His activities. The Church would prayerfully study them, test them, and ultimately choose a few from their number to certify as having been divinely inspired. Thus would come into existence what we call the canon of the New Testament.

Think about some of the dates. Mark and some of the early epistles would not be written until a generation after the ascension of Jesus to his heavenly Father. John's gospel, the last one accepted by the Church, would not be written until the very end of the first century. The various "books" would not be pulled together in the present format until the beginning of the fourth century, and by that time, thousands upon thousands of men and women had died for their faith in Jesus Christ without having ever seen or heard of the New Testament. So it is the Church that selects, codifies, and canonizes the New Testament.

If the Church was the determining factor in the formation of the New Testament, and the Christians accepted the Old Testament as God's sacred word, why did the Church not use the Bible more effectively in the thousand years from the fourth to the 20th century?

Let me make this clear: Bibles were produced by the thousands by hand, and then when printing became available in the 15th century, there were plenty to go around. It was therefore not physical scarcity, but the fact that the texts themselves were not made the central aspect of Christian living. That position was held by the sacraments. While the Church venerates the Bible and recognizes its importance, another force of life within the Church is the sacred mysteries. The Church believes these mysteries enable individuals to maintain direct contact with Jesus of Nazareth, and as such, to connect with all their brothers and sisters in the faith. *The sacraments make us one with Jesus and one with each other.*

During the Middle Ages, when the vast majority of the people were illiterate, the sacraments were the main contact with the living out of the faith. That caused a truly regrettable lapse in the utilization of God's Holy Word.

We should all be happy that there is a vigorous renewal of God's Holy Word taking place in the lives of individual Catholics and across the church all over the world, but so much remains to be done! Bible discussion clubs exist all across the land, but they need to be increased to the tens of thousands. Comfortable familiarity with the entire Bible, but especially the New Testament, is something that the Church must undertake in a much more vigorous way than it has since the council ended in 1965.

Today the ordinary Roman Catholic hears at Sunday Mass a three-year cycle with three scripture readings at each Sunday liturgy. This has helped greatly to familiarize Catholics in general with many of the more important texts. However, there are roughly six hundred New Testament texts; we hear only a third of the actual writings.

Each Sunday they are presented as a collage, with an underlying theme that brings to us a special message from our Lord to the community of faith, which is the Church.

Given, however, the size of the task before us, much more needs to be done.

It's important for Catholics to give serious thought to the ways in which they as individuals and as parishes could effectively utilize this precious gift, which comes directly from God. Let me say first what we should not do. It is foolish to open the Bible to chapter one, verse one, the book of Genesis, and begin to read straight through to the book of Revelations. You sometimes hear people brag that they have done this. There is nothing wrong with that, if you've got a lot of time on your hands, but it's not the best way to get a grasp on God's Holy Word.

Learn how to read the Bible! There is a simple skill that, if understood, makes reading sacred scripture far, far more enjoyable and productive. And that is to simply realize that the books of the Bible are many and varied, and read each section in its historical context.

Let me compare it to a newspaper. When you open the morning paper, the first section is national news, and the second section is local news. Your paper may have a section on cooking, crossword puzzles, business, sports, classified ads, and last but not least, the comics. No one has to be told that each one of those sections is written in a different literary form, and has to be read and evaluated on the basis of that literary form. You do not expect to be amused when you read the classified ads. You do not want to see the reporter's opinion worked into the news on page one. The editor's opinion is perfectly acceptable if it's limited to the editorial page. Different forms of writing have to be read differently, and this is true of the Bible.

The Bible contains a number of different genres: historical, biographical, poetic, theological, and even musical (hymns)—and of course these can be subdivided. For example, there are various types of history within the sacred text, and one must be conscious of exactly what one is reading. Not only does this marvelous book include many different literary styles, but also we know that many different people wrote the Bible, and the Bible may contain factual errors. This position is unacceptable, of course, to fundamentalists (including Catholic fundamentalists) who sincerely believe that the Holy Spirit directly dictated every word of the Bible and that it is free from error. *I want to stress that this view is not the position of the Catholic Church, which sees the Bible as inspired by God, but bringing messages to us through very human vehicles, namely the sacred authors.*

The best way to progress in spirituality is with a plan that includes prayer, meditation, spiritual reading, and spiritual direction. All of these are tools to bring us closer to Jesus, and the Bible should be paramount in this process. Needless to say, a systematic reading of the Bible would be a tremendous gift to one's daily prayer. How does one learn a productive approach to reading the Bible? Thankfully, we are blessed to have many small guidebooks on reading the New Testament. Any Catholic bookstore would have a number of alternative guides and plans from which to choose. If a person is intensely serious about developing a profound knowledge of the Sacred Text, then he or she should get a Biblical commentary. Again, there are many on the market from which to choose.

Once you have a clear understanding of how to read the Bible, then you can choose certain selections of readings that tie in with your ongoing journey in faith. For example, the epistles are tremendous aids in prayer and meditation. If someone were to pick up St. Paul's letter to the Corinthians, choose a certain section, read it, pray and reflect upon it and examine one's conscience in relationship to what St. Paul is calling us to do, this would be a tremendous asset to your journey.

Let's view the Bible as a precious gift from God—a gift that is both valuable and pragmatic, and a gift that is actually a tool to growing closer to Jesus of Nazareth. As we use this tool, this gift, after a period of time we will be able to say, like St. Paul, "I live now not I, but Christ lives in me."

HOW MUCH CHURCH IS ENOUGH?

"Keep Holy the Sabbath Day."

—God

"Attend Mass on Sundays and Holy Days of obligation."
—the Church and the Pope

"John, get up, we have to go to Mass."
—Bishop McCarthy's mother

Laws, laws, laws. We can't belong to a political entity, a church, or a fraternal organization without coming up against laws and policies that put obligations upon us.

The most fundamental laws are universal for the human family, and they bind everyone, everywhere at all times. These have been collated in the Jewish tradition in what we call the Ten Commandments, but essentially, they are horse-sense rules, which originate from our human nature.

It's natural to avoid killing people. It is natural to want to pay tribute to some greater force that we don't understand, but that we believe has caused our existence. It's natural to want to protect our property in order to provide ourselves and our families with the means of survival. Those laws are universal. They bind everybody at all times.

We are also faced with civil laws, which many times are simply applications of the divine law. There is no civilized society that doesn't forbid the killing of innocent people. When you kill an innocent person, you are guilty of murder. So, civil society has these laws, and really, many more laws than we are given from God.

Under divine law, and in addition to civic law, we Catholics belong to a church that really stresses legality. The church does this for the same reason that the civil society does, because good laws promulgated properly and enforced consistently protect people's freedom. So, good laws maintained in that fashion are a real asset to the society and the individual.

Among the many laws that the church places before us is the obligation of Sunday Mass attendance. How this is carried out varies in different parts of the world. The natural tendency to worship a higher power has to take place even in the distant Andes Mountains. The Church law (that we have to attend Mass on Sunday) cannot possibly be fulfilled by millions of people—such as South Americans—who have access to Mass only once per year. There is only one priest for roughly every 25,000 people in that region, which obviously precludes weekly attendance for all.

In the United States, the obligation of Sunday Mass has been taken very seriously by the Roman Catholic community. Prior to the second Vatican council, on any given Sunday, probably seventy to seventy-five percent of Catholics in any specified region would be at Mass on Sunday. We built these big churches, and had Mass every hour on the hour each Sunday. Sometimes the crowds would be so big that people would get in line outside the church, and slowly file through as Mass was said continuously, with up to ten priests hearing confessions on the sides of the church.

One of the by-products of the council—not necessarily intended—was considerable relaxation as far as church law is concerned. You don't hear priests preaching that eating meat on Fridays in Lent is a grave sin, which would possibly cause your eternal damnation. You don't hear priests saying that to miss Mass on Sunday is a grave sin, although they will say that attending is a grave obligation. With that different stance, people are still going to church by the millions, but not everyone. My guess is that now, in any given month, only 50-60% of self-described Catholics have been to church at least once during the month. There is not the same pressure to attend Mass that there once was.

In my opinion, that measure of relaxation is a good thing because we're no longer going to church out of fear. Now, people are going to church because they want to be there. The problem is that in so many of the Roman Catholic churches, services often seem to be too casual, lacking in proper respect. One of the greatest problems in our Church is inadequate preaching. In fact, sometimes it's not just inadequate, it's disastrous. Another problem area is the music. Resources for the sacred music are often inadequate as well—but we do need to enhance the songs we are offering as we worship God.

If the Church wants to get its inactive members back, to increase the faithful at the Sunday Mass attendance, we must be concerned about the quality of the liturgy in general, the enhancement of sacred music, and finding some way to improve the quality of preaching. *What could be done?* Perhaps there could be a small committee in the parish with the task of evaluating Sunday homilies, and giving the priest their views on how he could improve. Not to micromanage, but to offer constructive feedback on delivery or reflections on what they took home from the sermon (so the priest could see how that compares to his intent). This intervention, of course, would need to be tied in with massive re-education of the clergy as far as public speaking and preaching is concerned.

Preaching is an art, and one that can be learned. There are some priests that are too shy, or so burdened by stage fright that they will never be effective preachers, but for most, it's something that can be learned. If the preaching in the Catholic Church is considered a disaster by a large portion of the Church, then the Church, if it wants to take itself seriously and be taken seriously, has to enhance the quality of its preaching.

Let's go back to church attendance. Even in the pre-Vatican Council days, we had two things that freed parishioners from the obligation of Sunday Mass. One was a dispensation—the Church, through the pastor or occasionally the bishop, could exercise their jurisdiction to say that members were relieved of the obligation of that law that day. The other was an excusing cause. An excusing cause, especially today, would be a long journey on Sunday morning, a sick relative, relatives unexpectedly visiting, working, or being sick. These were considered an "excusing cause", thus relieving the obligation for Mass that day, and these two options have been around for over 150 years.

Does television Mass "count"? No. Mass is not a show or a theatre. When we are at Mass, we are with the community, and Jesus is in the community. Watching Mass projected over a television screen is a consolation for those who are sick and cannot get to Mass. Let's hope if someone is on a T.V. Mass that the homily is well prepared.

Do we need to go to church? Well, yes! The key verb there is NEED. We naturally need to acknowledge the source of our existence. That's why uncivilized tribes have always and everywhere worshiped one or more beings or gods that they thought were the source of their existence. It's natural. We are naturally loving and respectful of our parents because they gave us existence. There is an inner thrust for a person to express appreciation for our existence, for family, for home and joy, and perhaps an occasional scotch whiskey. So yes, we need to express our appreciation to our God.

What the Church has done is specify a minimum of respect and adoration that we should offer our Heavenly Father. It doesn't say that going to Mass every day is not a wonderful thing—many people do, and that's marvelous for them—but there is no obligation there. What the Church does ask for is a *minimum*. For most people, this time of worship is in the morning of the first day of the week. It's the first thing that you do, and it ties in with the Eucharistic fast. You go to Mass to begin the week. The most important thing you do at Mass is to receive the Eucharist, the real presence of Jesus. What a great way to start the week! Let's go to Mass.

PRAYER

"You can outlaw prayer in schools, but trust me, come test day
—it will be there!"

Prayer is an important part of a person's religious and faith life. Prayer takes many forms, and we each utilize it in different ways. I have to admit that my favorite and most-used form is that of petition. I am frequently bringing various problems and difficulties to God's attention, and indicating with great clarity what it is exactly that He should bring about—and on my time schedule, of course.

Seriously, though, prayer is an important word in the lives of most people who profess to have faith, but it is a word with a wide variety of meanings. In general, it is the way we manifest in our own personal lives how we do or want to relate to the God that we worship.

I would like to start by stressing two aspects of prayer. One, that prayer is a universal reality in the lives of believing people. Two, there is no particular form or manifestation that is superior to another. There is no simple straight way that is the "correct" way to pray.

While believers depend on prayer as a source of strength and a cause of encouragement, they approach it in as many different ways as there are believers. Having said that, we can still describe various customs, traditions, or habits of prayer that different people practice.

Catholics have the reputation, not completely deserved, as praying constantly from formulas of prayer, such as the Lord's Prayer, the Rosary, the Apostle's Creed, and various types of novenas. This does not mean that Catholics do not also pray in a completely ad-libbed manner; it's just that when they come together, there is a rich tradition of common prayer. This is true when they attend Mass, conventions, and whenever large numbers of Catholics unite. Whether it's 200 or 200,000 Catholics simultaneously uniting their voices in prayer, in my opinion that's a beautiful manifestation of shared faith. However, I must say that it doesn't provide the same type of personal satisfaction that comes from an intensely personal prayer directed at God by one believing heart, concerning his or her hopes, dreams, wants, needs, and fears, etc.

Catholics love to define things. It's part of the influence of Aristotelian philosophy in our story. We love to define. We define what we define, and then we re-define it, lest there be some confusion about the meanings.

In the area of prayer, we tend to classify prayers into four general categories. In my opinion, the categories are logical, but do not begin to cover all the various approaches to prayer. Those categories are: *Adoration, Petition, Thanksgiving, and Contrition.*

The words speak for themselves.

One of the reasons we are here as creatures of God is that we would contribute to His glory by worship. We don't just acknowledge that there is a supreme being; we pay humble tribute to the awesome reality which is Godness. Look at the words we use: infinite knowledge, infinite love, and infinite this and that. We use those words, and we believe and mean those words, but our minds really can't grasp the word "infinite" by itself, let alone all the infinite qualities that are present in God. In a nutshell, when we are conscious of Who and What God is, and we are conscious of our own inadequacy and finiteness, the response ought to be adoration. This is a natural human response in the face of something that awes us. We feel it gazing into the Grand Canyon, or admiring an extraordinarily beautiful sunset, and we feel it when we look at the tiny feet of a newborn baby. Thinking about God generates awe, and awe challenges us to bring forth adoration. This may be the form of prayer that we use the least.

The second type of prayer, petition, comes more easily. We know in our day-to-day life that we want things, and there is a smaller list of things that we need. Usually, in our prayer we mix these together all too easily! "Give me this, get me that, help me with this." We're asking God, because we believe in our faith that God is all-powerful, and might respond positively to that for which we are asking if it is truly for our benefit.

Prayer of petition seems simple enough, doesn't it? We want something, and we ask God to bring it about or to help us to bring it about. Here it's important to realize that God does not routinely run the world with miracles. If something is within our talents, responsibilities, or capabilities, then WE have to use those talents and knowledge to bring about our request. It's true that we ask God to help us, but we realize that just the act of asking is a help, because we become more clearly conscious of our own limitations and strengths. We know that ultimately, everything happens according to God's will.

When a doctor walks into a surgical suite and asks God for guidance that sharpens her mind, she is effectively praying. There are contingency factors that are out of human control. He or she may be the most skilled surgeon in the world, but may not conduct a particular operation in the best way without God's help. We really are asking God's help to be able to use the gifts He's given us to our ultimate ability.

Bringing prayer closer to home, let me give you an example of one way I pray. People come to see me because they are distraught or discouraged, or even physically in danger. They may have very serious issues in the home or in their business. Before I meet with them the first time, I ask God to help me to use as effectively as possible the gifts that I do have—whatever those gifts are that might help the person coming to see me.

Usually, the gift is that of a lot of experience—over a half a century of dealing with thousands of human problems—many of which are similar and require comparable responses, while others continue to be totally unique. I'll ask God to help me to distinguish in my mind the best choice of advice or guidance for this person. Through that very process, I'm reminded of what my strengths and gifts from God really are, which already helps me to focus more clearly on the problem at hand.

Let's get back to the different forms of prayer. The third form is thanksgiving, and it should go hand-in-glove with petition, because we should be instinctively thankful when the things that we desired are placed within our reach. It's a funny thing about humans, though. The petition comes easily, but thanksgiving is often lost in the flow of life's excitement. Jesus himself had this problem with the ten lepers who were cured: only one returned to say thank you. It's a human problem, and will therefore always be part of our story.

The last category is the prayer of contrition. I'm happy to say that this comes almost as easily as petition. Nature has blessed the vast majority of us with a conscience, and when we do something that's really wrong, we instinctively move to regret it and to commit ourselves to avoiding that mistake in the future. The fact that the Sacrament of Penance is celebrated every Saturday in the Church is a reflection of the fact that not all of these good intentions are easily fulfilled. *I like to remind people that God deals with us as though life were a tennis game, not a golf game.* In golf, your mistakes are written down and held against you 'til the end of the round. In tennis, you forget the mistake and enjoy an endless series of new beginnings. We all fall, and we all make mistakes. We experience contrition and start over.

What must never be forgotten and always stressed is that prayer is conversation with God. Conversation! That conversation must be *natural* from the point of view of the person that is doing the praying. This opens up the need for personal, non-memorized prayer. I believe the only advantage of memorized prayer is making it easy to pray aloud together. We tend to get into a format that we're comfortable with, and use it repeatedly. Instead, I think we should struggle to avoid that, and get back to the concept of an ongoing, personal conversation with our Lord.

O COME, O COME, EMMANUEL

"Advent is concerned with that very connection between memory and hope which is so necessary to man. Advent's intention is to awaken the most profound and basic emotional memory within us, namely, the memory of the God who became a child... It is the beautiful task of Advent to awaken in all of us memories of goodness and thus to open doors of hope."
—*Cardinal Joseph Ratzinger (from Seek That Which is Above- 1986)*

The Catholic Church is probably one of the most interesting institutions on the planet. It's old, it's big, and it's cumbersome. Our Church has lots of strengths, and God knows it has weaknesses. *Some of the strengths, though, come from the wisdom of centuries.* One thing that the Church has sort of stumbled into is the idea of running an annual cycle of its principal beliefs.

The Church's goal is to present the message of Jesus to all of its members, young and old alike. To accomplish this, it has developed a number of different age-appropriate methods. Children often learn initially about Jesus from the joy and fun of Christmas and Easter celebrations. Most of our youth are enrolled in a program of religious education especially adapted for their needs, based upon age-appropriate explanations of our faith. Older students may deepen that understanding through the more serious study of theology.

Throughout history, formal educational venues such as these and other efforts have been utilized to present the message of our Church, but the most important source of formation and education remains the liturgy of the Church. The artistic and emotional aspects of the Church's liturgy affect the majority of participating adults.

Every year, the liturgy presents the whole story of the history of salvation, beginning with Cain and Abel and extending through the feast of Christ the King, which closes the Church year. In my opinion, the Liturgical year is one of the really great strengths of our Church, and for me, it's not just built on theology and Church history, but also on good psychology.

Human beings love anticipation. We just love to anticipate, because the unknown is mysterious, and tomorrow is unknown. So, any time we have a chance to look forward to something, we find ourselves pushed forward by enthusiasm and hope. Of course, mostly we like to look forward to things that are pleasant; we don't like to look forward to something that is potentially painful. So because of that principle, the Church sticks Advent in the beginning of the year—it has you looking ahead.

One other thing about the Church is that it loves contrast. Christmas is joyful, vibrant, and beautiful. Advent, if enforced as it used to be, is rather dreary. You don't have flowers. You're really not supposed to have music. All you get out of advent is some extra prayers. BUT, if all the way through that four-week period you're thinking, "Something's coming. Don't worry about today being dreary—something is coming." And then with Christmas, it comes! There's that explosive celebration, and it overflows into the world, and people celebrate in a very special way. That's the background on Advent.

Now, I think that another aspect of Advent is that in the traditional advent, you were getting ready for the future. You were encouraged not to be worrying about the mistakes of today, or the problems of today, but the great thing that's coming. We need that in our own individual lives in a very special way. We need to always be able—or at least we need to try to be able—to be looking forward to something that is good. Maybe it's just a scotch and water at 5 p.m.; maybe it's a walk in the park. But putting pleasant things ahead of us is not only pleasant, but it gives us motivation that we need to keep moving forward.

The way our mind works is that if we want to develop ourselves to be more optimistic, or more organized, then we have to *systematically be putting goals in front of ourselves.* We need goals that are attractive to us; goals that we want to achieve. And when we do that, we have to modulate the way we function. If I want to take off fifteen pounds, I may have to skip the pasta or dessert (*but perhaps I don't want to take them off that badly.*) If we set goals, and if we have the willpower to make the decisions on what's necessary to achieve those goals, then it will affect our conduct, day by day.

And so if you step back, then, from the Liturgical year, and you look at Advent, you see it not just as a pious custom or a batch of purple on the Church calendar, but an opportunity to grow and develop spiritually, and but physically and psychologically as well. I'm all for Advent!

LISTENING TO MARY

"And the angel said to her, Do not be afraid, Mary, for you have found favor with God. And behold, you will conceive in your womb and bear a son, and you shall call his name Jesus. For with God, nothing shall be impossible."

—Luke 1:30-31 and 1:37

Many differences exist between the various manifestations of Christianity, although we're far closer than most people realize. One of the big differences between Roman Catholicism and other mainline churches like the Presbyterians, Methodists, and Baptists (and less so with Anglicans and Lutherans) is the role that Mary plays in Roman Catholic devotion and in Roman Catholic theology—*and there's a big difference.* Mary is extraordinarily powerful in Roman Catholic devotion. She is important in Roman Catholic theology, mainly because Mary has manifested herself since the second century (that we know of, and presumably in the first century as well).

Let me start with some concerns. There are those outside the Catholic Church that have accused us for centuries of Mary-idolatry. They're not all completely wrong. There was a near heresy only twenty-five or thirty years ago. There was a large push from vocal minority within Catholic circles for the Church to define that "all grace comes to us through Mary"—that Jesus achieved it, but Mary is the vehicle, the funnel. Their view was that Mary is side by side with Jesus for our redemption, and I think that's heresy.

Marian devotion has a long history. Let's go back to the Church in the fourth and fifth centuries, and pick up again with early modern times. Jesus of Nazareth is the center of our faith. Jesus is our Redeemer. It is through Jesus that we go to our redemption, to the Father. However, once it was clarified that Jesus was both God and man- that He was divine- this concept overpowered the spiritual lives of the people. That's true—in our faith, that's true: God is here. Jesus, God, is divine. There's nothing wrong with being down on your knees. But if it reaches the point where we can't talk to him as a brother, we've lost something. And then Jesus becomes more and more remote.

The purpose of the Incarnation is the infleshment of our salvation; *that we can see the person, the vehicle through which we are moving towards our Heavenly Father.* As Jesus became more and more recessed into the great Cathedrals, higher and higher up there; His wonderful mother began to come to the forefront. And she, then, fulfilled this accessible role in the prayer life of the people.

We often stress Jesus' divinity to the point where we forget His humanity. We accept Mary's humanity, however. She's something we can understand: a young girl, a woman, a mother- a mother who has lost a child. Those are all things that we can understand. When we make the Stations of the Cross, and we see that Mary looks at Jesus in His filth and dirt and bloodiness, our hearts usually don't go out to Jesus at the time, they go out to her. Poor woman! Why is this happening to her?

The second Vatican council has brought greater clarity to Marian devotion. Are we saying she wasn't the mother of God? Mother of His human nature? Mother of a human being who was also God? No! Of course she was and is all those things. These are expressions that I'm very comfortable with, and I've only had them for the last forty years—I didn't have them as a kid. We used to have numerous Marian litanies: Star of the Sea, Tower of Ivory; nothing wrong with them, they are beautiful poetic expressions to say how wonderful Mary is.

The greatest thing that we can say for Mary after we say that she is the mother of Jesus, is that she is the mother of the Church. Mary is the last person in the Old Testament, and the first person in the New Testament. She's a bridge between yesterday and tomorrow. That's a tremendous relationship! Jesus comes out of Mary the way Jesus comes out of the Church. In other words, there's a point in time where there is just Mary, and no Church. Then there is a point in time when Jesus arrives, and the Church begins. Mary is in between, that bridge from the old to the new. I may only be able to defend that poetically, not theologically, but that's how I see it.

In modern times, we honor Mary tremendously, and this adoration manifests itself often. For example, when I was in office, there were 125 parishes, and about thirty of them were named after Mary. We haven't backed off in honoring Mary.

I think that our handling of the blessed Eucharist—literally taking the host in our hands, which makes it more like food, and the procession—we all process together on our journey and share this food from heaven—this is much more realistic than kneeling on both knees in worship. Again, if someone wants to kneel down, that's fine; it's their business. But, all these little things collectively have brought the Eucharist, the real presence of Jesus of Nazareth, much closer to us in our day-to-day lives. I think that's a very good thing. Therefore, we love Mary, the mother of the Lord. We recognize her greatness, but we're not as dependent on her in our spiritual life and in the way we journey spiritually. I'm very comfortable talking to Jesus. I think He's got wonderful hearing.

Much has been built around the marriage feast of Cana. "They have no wine." "What is that to me and to thee? My hour has not yet come." And Mary says, "Do what He tells you." *I agree. Let's listen to her.*

WOMEN IN THE CHURCH

"We have to begin dealing with the larger half of our membership dif- ferently than we have been since the dawn of time. The Church's posi- tion is, by my standards, inadequate as far as women are concerned. However, in fairness to the Church, the whole society has only been addressing this inequity for around a hundred years. A woman who lived in Texas when I was born couldn't even buy a piece of property, couldn't get a credit card."
— *Bishop John McCarthy*

What is the role of women in the Church? To ask this is to ask a very down- to-earth question, and yet at the same time, to open Pandora's Box. The reason I say that is that there's no one single role for women within the Church, just as there is no one single role for a woman in the larger societ- ies that cover this planet.

Let's address the history first.

Throughout human history, women have had the role imposed upon them of being vulnerable and dependent. The prime reason for this is that the role of childbearing belongs to women alone, which automati- cally brings with it a certain role of dependence. While pregnant, a woman must be very careful to protect the baby within her body, and then once the baby is born, traditionally the role of the care of that child descends on the shoulders of the woman, which of course made it difficult for her to hunt or be effective in warfare. Since those were the two main occupations of the adult males in primitive society—hunting and fighting—it's obvious why the woman's role became looked upon as inferior and dependent.

Happily, that situation has changed over the last several centuries. While individual women, even as far back as a couple thousand years ago (I think of Cleopatra), have risen to positions of power in a variety of countries or times, the vast majority of women throughout time have lived under conditions where they are considered inferior. We can all give thanks that this situation has been gradually changing! Yes, women are still bearing children—the alternatives are somewhat limited—but an ever-increasing number of women have received education, which has broadened their opportunities. Many women now have an increased share in power. Today there are complaints that there are so few women in charge of Fortune 500 companies. My goodness, what a terrific marker of change! It was inconceivable even fifty years ago that people would complain that there were not enough women running these enormous corporations. Now we are justifiably upset that there are not more of them!

With greater education, better job opportunities, the gradual disintegration of the glass ceiling, and the tremendous increase in political power, we've seen the role of women (at least in the West) changing at a steady pace, and that change is ongoing. Recently, a woman was nearly nominated for the office of President. All this, however, is the secular society in the West.

The situation is not the same in the Roman Catholic Church. In the Catholic Church, there are many different roles, responsibilities, and ministries, but in point of fact, there is not a woman in the Roman Catholic Church that has real power. Power in the Catholic Church is called "ordinary power." It comes from the Greek word meaning "muscle." No one can exercise ordinary power in the Roman Catholic Church except a man. This is brought about without any reference to women as such, but the fact is that all power is in the hands of the pastor, the Bishop, and the Bishop of Rome (the Pope). These are all males who have achieved anointing to the priesthood or papacy. All power in the Catholic Church is in the hands of ordained males.

Does this mean women do not have influence? Not at all—no more than it did in Cleopatra's time. There are women who run hospitals and universities, raise millions of dollars, and are extraordinary academics. However, the actual exercise of power in the life of the Church is denied them. This distinction may seem far-fetched, but it is a very important distinction.

What should be done? There is a whole movement in various cultures and social systems toward enhancement of the role of women and creating true equality for women with their male counterparts. All you have to do is look at the movement of the last two hundred years to see that we are steadily moving toward enhancing the role of women in our secular society. Women are advancing in education, wealth, politics, and power. BUT, this is not happening in the Church.

It's a great thing that we are coming into a new period of human history where women are throwing over the shackles that held them down. Now, the people who differ with my view would say that women have been "protected," and that they've been on a pedestal. But I don't think women want to be on a pedestal!

No female can hold power in the ecclesiastical sense in the Roman Catholic Church. She may have tremendous influence—if a woman is president of a liberal arts college with 10,000 students, for example, that's a lot of influence. But she has no power inside the church. The little monsignor down the street has more church power than she does. To have a church of somewhere around a billion members, with more than half of them female, and not a single one of them possessing any *ordinary power*—to use the technical term—in my view, that is substantially in error at this time in history!

Is there a theological reason to justify denying women the right to share in power in the Church? Not at all, says a major group of scripture scholars, who studied this issue and delivered the Catholic Biblical Society's opinion, saying, "There is no reason in scripture to block the ordination of women."

That position paper did not please authorities in the Vatican, and they continue their position unchanged, which is that while saying sweet, loving things about females, they will not consider sharing ordinary power.

Again, what should be done? For those of us who believe in a certain inevitability in history, you don't have to do anything. The change is coming, and will likely arrive just as fast with or without a huge, aggressive fight. There are however, groups organized within the Catholic community to advance the cause of the ordination of women. The most outspoken is called the Women's Ordination Conference. They call for the ordination of women, and they've had a number of religious ceremonies where women are "ordained." Once again, this produces strong negative reactions from Church authorities.

Where do I stand? First of all, I'm a practicing Catholic, and want to live my life within the Church. *Therefore, I cannot push for what would be a profound revolutionary step in the administrative life of the Church.* If that change comes about, it will need to come about through the efforts of those who have ordinary power. The good news is that even within my life-time, we have seen many examples of this. Do you remember when women could not wash the altar cloths? A priest had to wash them first, in case there was a speck of the Host on them. Women could not read scripture in Church, nor be parish administrators. *There are a whole host of changes in the Church.* I don't think anyone can say with absolute confidence that change will not prevail so that women will be ordained. I believe, however, that the current approach of the Women's Ordination Conference is very unlikely to succeed.

What will the future hold? Let's pray, wait, and see.

THE HOLY SPIRIT

"We believe that the Holy Spirit dwells within that community, but not that He micro-manages it on a daily basis."
—Bishop John McCarthy

One of the most difficult concepts in Christian theology is that the vast majority of Christians believe that within the nature of God, there are several relationships that are so complete and so perfect that we end up calling them "persons." That's hard to grasp. We believe that there is one God, and within that God there are three relationships—distinct and yet, at the same time, one. What we often do when we can't see or explain something is we say, "That's a mystery". George Carlin made that line famous when he was just getting started thirty years ago. He said that every time the Catholic Church has a problem that it can't explain, it says, "Well, it's a mystery!" Well, in this case, actually, it is.

Instead of talking straight about God, let's lay some limitations out on the table. My brain and your brain are very limited. Yours may be very brilliant, and mine may be much more limited, but the fact is that they are both truly limited. When we turn around and start talking about God—just using words—we use those words to describe an infinite power that is the cause of all existence. This power continues to sustain everything in existence. Part of its power is established in a relationship with these special beings, the human beings, which it created.

When we say eternal, or infinite, *we can't grasp experientially what those words really mean.* Therefore, you start off with the fact that while the human brain can deduce certain things in relationship to God, or project certain things—like when we say God is eternal or infinitely merciful, we're only projecting. We take a very human concept and put "infinite" in front of it. So we say I'm smart, he's smart, she's smart, but God is "infinitely smart." We can't truly grasp that.

It has been believed by the Christian community since the first century that within the divine essence, within what we call "god-ness" or God, there are three distinctions that manifest themselves. That concept had never been held before. This is a uniquely Christian concept, although Christians will argue that manifestations appear in the book of Genesis. There, the sacred author has God speaking as "we." He breathed into Adam a living soul: the breath, the Spirit.

The first person has paternity, creativity, and power, and we call Him God the Father. We don't know much about the second person of the blessed trinity until Jesus begins to reveal His divine nature. He says, "I have come forth from the Father." Jesus slowly reveals to His apostles that He is a real human being. They'll see nails go through His hands. They'll see His back lacerated from a whip. That's very human. But, He also has always been there. "In the beginning was the Word, and the Word was with God, and the Word was God." That's Greek philosophy at work there. St. Mark's Gospel is very clear and direct that the Jews of that day were not into philosophy; let's state the facts. "This is the gospel of Jesus Christ, the Son of God." Bang! That's the beginning of his gospel.

You can't just start talking about the Holy Spirit. There were lots of spirits before the coming of Jesus. There wasn't any group of people on the planet that believed in only one god. That would be absurd. The rivers have gods; the skies have gods. There are gods that cause sickness, and gods that heal. Gods are everywhere, and they're all spirits. Then Jesus comes along and says, "I have come forth from the Father." Then He says who He is. Then He introduces this third entity. "I have many things to say to you, but you cannot bear them now. The Father and I will send you the spirit of truth, who will bring to your mind whatsoever I have commanded you." He sends them out. "Go forth into the whole world. Teach them everything that I have commanded you, baptizing them (washing them, literally) in the name of the Father, and of the Son, and of the Holy Spirit." Jesus tells the apostles that when He returns to His Father, "Don't get upset. We will send the Spirit to you."

The Acts of the Apostles then describes how all the disciples are gathered, and with a tremendous display of power, their lives are transformed. They go from being shy and insecure to becoming very brave persons guided by the Spirit. Visually, they saw a fire coming out of the sky and spreading out over the head of each person there.

That is the Holy Spirit.

Christian tradition humanizes a divinity. The Father is the Creator. The Son is the Redeemer. The Holy Spirit is the Sanctifier—He's the one who makes us holy.

When we calmly pray, and turn our hearts and minds to God, it's the spirit of God that's transforming us and lifting us up. We believe strongly in the Trinity, the three natures, one God. Jesus revealed it, and the Church has taught it since the first generation. But it's hard to get your brain around the Holy Spirit.

God, an infinitely powerful being, is not too difficult. We don't have to see that. We project that, and picture him sitting on a throne with a long grey beard, holding a scepter. He's bigger, higher, in a bigger chair. He's wise, so he's old.

Then Jesus, He's easy. When you start talking to me about a Jewish carpenter, I can understand that. When you talk about him dying, or crying, or eating, or creating six huge vats of wine on the third day of a party, I can really understand those things. But when you talk to me about the Spirit, it's nebulous, because, well, it's a spirit!

Then, the Church says they are all equal. The Holy Spirit is equal to God the Father and God the Son. This simply doesn't make sense to us. Human beings have a natural tendency to prioritize. So, if there is a father, fathers are more important than sons. The Father has got to be in our psychological reaction more important than the Son. If you look at the Apostle's Creed, which was written in the first century, it says, "I believe in God the Father, Creator of Heaven and Earth, and in Jesus Christ, His son." Then, way down, we finally address the Holy Spirit. There is controversy: what does this mean? In the year 312, the bishops gathered and the Nicene Creed was born—around six clauses describing the relationship between the Father and the Son.

There has been a resurgence of interest in and devotion to the Holy Spirit over the last hundred years. It's not that people stopped believing in it, but now there's a need in the Church to feel the presence of God in a very special formative way. Whether or not this is accurate doesn't matter. The Church has assigned the gifts of the spirit—the gifts of inspiring people, encouraging people, enlightening people, guidance—all the gifts we all really need, to the Holy Spirit. There is a tiny speck of humility coming through the back door of the Catholic Church, recognizing that we must receive these gifts from God. It's a comforting thing.

It's infinitely mysterious that there are relationships inside of God that for lack of a better word, we call "persons." That does not mean that they are the same as those we mean when we say "persons." It means "distinct identity". There's a relationship between these three realities within God. With our natural curiosity, we want an answer, but we won't get one on earth. If we'd get used to the idea that we're not going to get answers—and even if we did, we wouldn't understand them—we'd all be a lot calmer.

LENT

"Nobody's afraid of Lent anymore!"
— *Bishop John McCarthy*

When I was young, and the church bulletin and the announcements would bring forth the declaration that next Sunday would mark the beginning of Lent, many Catholics would shiver and quake in their shoes. *That was Lent before the second Vatican council.*

Some of the practices that were required were moderately difficult, and since so many of us are weak in facing difficulties, even moderate ones produce fear. The laws of fasting and abstinence were quite strict. No meat on Wednesday and Friday; only one full meal for adults; no snacking between meals; and of course people would add their own private penances such as no movies, no candy, etc. It probably would have been better if we had eaten the candy and given up gossiping instead!

First, however, what is the purpose of Lent? You can't get at the purpose of Lent without talking about a more fundamental issue, that is, the Church's liturgical year. This special year, around which our spiritual lives should be ordered, has as its purpose to present in front of us every fifty-two weeks the whole story of God's love for the human family. That story begins with Adam and Eve, and carries through until the end of time marked in the Church year by the feast of Christ the King.

In between, the Church year is a rollercoaster. It goes down. It comes up. It goes down again and then back up. Finally, there is a long and somewhat uneventful period.

Lent is the second trip down. It isn't really "down", of course, it's just that it seems that way to us because we find ourselves doing things that are slightly unpleasant. Lent is a six-week period in which the Church urges us to practice, much more than is usually the case, a program of discipline and good works. Traditionally the discipline has been some type of denial in one form or another. I believe, however, that the good works are much more important.

Let's imagine two people are riding in a bus. One has decided to not eat candy, and the other is going out of his way to help a fellow student who is abused or misunderstood. In my opinion, the person reaching out to lessen the pain in the life of another is doing something more important than the modest pain experienced by a stomach that is craving chocolate and being denied.

Lent is a gift, a wonderful gift that helps us put life in a clearer context. Each day finds us very distracted and pulled in different directions. If we discipline ourselves during Lent to begin and end the day with prayer; to, in a very determined way, be more generous and sensitive to others; to give some of our wealth (whether it be quarters or large checks) to programs that lessen pain; then we're really getting ready to spiritually march up Calgary Hill with Jesus on Good Friday.

If we follow Jesus up that hill, and in some very limited way experience the suffering of the cross, then we are marvelously prepared and ready and even exuberant for the explosive joy of the Resurrection. There is absolutely no need to fear or dread this season. Let's hear it for Lent!

THE ART OF RECONCILIATION

*"We don't teach that anybody is in hell. We teach that
there is a hell, because the essence of hell is separation from God. But
the Catholic Church has no idea whether any specific is there."*
— *Bishop John McCarthy*

After my ordination in May of 1956, I was given three weeks' vacation. Being very eager to begin to exercise priestly ministry, however, I volunteered to cover a pastor in a small town in the diocese who wanted to go on vacation. I went out there, and at that time confessions were scheduled from 4-6pm and again from 7-9pm.

I can still remember what an awesome experience it is to be seated behind a curtain in a confessional and have your fellow human beings on their knees admitting to this or that failure. While I was profoundly moved by that early experience, I must say in all honesty that I was even more impressed by the very narrow range of human weakness. I think I can say that after those first four hours were over in that small country town south of Houston, I really have never heard anything new in the confessional.

The sacrament of penance, and the way in which we celebrate it, has changed dramatically since I was ordained over fifty-two years ago. We changed the name. We've changed the manner in which is handled logistically, and to a certain extent, we've changed what we accent in the celebration of the sacrament.

In 1956, Catholics went to CONFESSION. It was a sort of reporting in to God to let Him know that things had not gone perfectly well since the last time that we were there.

Today, most Catholics do not routinely go to Confession. They know that God has known of their mistakes, not just from the instant that they occurred, but from all eternity. So, what we're actually doing in Confession is being reconciled to the Church. *That's really an awesome difference and emphasis.* It's restoring the practice of Confession, Penance, and Reconciliation back to the way it was celebrated in the very early Church.

The early Christians had a strong bond to their community of faith, and they realized that when they failed—by sin, or by denial of Christ, or some other serious human weakness—that they were weakening the community. This was especially true in the early centuries in terms of the practice of turning away from a commitment to Christ and worshipping false gods such as the Roman emperor. They felt very strongly that they had not just offended God, but that they had betrayed their brothers and sisters in faith.

The early Catholics would come to the Church, and in the presence of the community (and their communities were quite small) they would admit they had failed in the practice of their faith. They would admit that they had denied their faith in Jesus Christ, or they would admit some serious other moral offense. They would admit it in the middle of the community, and most especially to the person who was presiding—the one we call the priest—although they would not have used that terminology. Then the priest, in the name of the community, would impose a penance; some type of disciplinary action that would, in some limited fashion, atone for the offense against the community. A common means was to deny the person participation in the Eucharistic celebration for a year or two. Such people would come to church on Sunday morning and kneel at the entrance of whatever place they were utilizing, whatever the sacred area was, and as people were passing by they would say, "Please pray for me, for I am a sinner." When the Eucharist started, they would be sent home, since they were not allowed to participate until the end of their prescribed period of penance. Can you imagine?

By the fourth or fifth century, Christians were beginning to see that the punishment didn't really have to be this tough. Then- and I think this part is funny—they picked up the whole ceremony, kit and caboodle, and moved it from Sunday morning in front of the congregation to Saturday night in back of the church. For most of us who went to Confession before the liturgical changes of the last half- century, this is how it looked. You would go into a darkened church, wait in line for your turn until you could enter the confessional, and on bended knee whisper your faults and disappointments in yourself and in your failures; receive a penance—sometimes extraordinarily difficult—like saying three Hail Mary's; go back outside and say an act of contrition, and go home with a tremendous sense of relief.

Today's system is much better theology. We accent that God knows everything about us from all eternity. We don't need to inform Him, but what we do need is a sense that our failures as followers of Jesus set the Church back. Who knows how big the Church would be today if it were not for our sinfulness, our failures, and our disobedience?

Another difference in the way the Sacrament of Penance (Reconciliation) is celebrated today from that of fifty years ago is that penitents are given the option of face-to-face "confession." On a personal note, I'm amazed that most people prefer this to the dark of the shrouded confessional!

Another change is that people do not feel a compulsive need to go to the sacrament of penance frequently. I think it's a good thing that we have a little clearer understanding that sin is not as pervasive in our lives as the Irish Church of the 19th century made us think. We talk less about sin, but when we do talk about it, it tends to be far more serious. We've scrapped the idea that every little mistake is a sin. For example, let me clarify that if one doesn't say his or her prayers in the morning or evening, that is not a *sin*. We *should* pray, but to *not* pray is not a sin. We had the overly sensitive idea that any imperfections were sins, and should be reported. I'm glad we're past that.

So, how often should we celebrate the Sacrament of Penance? The Church says once per year, but even that mild obligation only binds if you think that you are in grave sin. The Church would like priests and nuns to do an examination of conscience twice per day. That's a lot for the average person, but at least once a day or once a month, stop and reflect on your attitudes and behavior. Strictly speaking, there is no obligation to go to the Sacrament of Penance. That's one of the old laws of the Church. After all, who goes a year without a big sin? Therefore, if it's been a year, you need to go (says the old Irish Church). Remember what they used to do? Go to Confession just before Easter Sunday, then hurry up and go to Communion before you commit another sin!

There is something wonderful about how we celebrate this Sacrament today.

The majority of us give ourselves credit for being right most of the time. Preparing for the Sacrament of Reconciliation requires that we give up the safety of self-righteousness, and look at ourselves and objectively review the Commandments and the virtues. Remember, we don't have to confess imperfections. However, as we get ready for the Sacrament of Reconciliation, it is wonderful for us to go through the exercise of examining our lives. *How is my faith? How is my charity? Am I really a person of hope?*

In this inquisition, you are the district attorney, and there is no one there to defend you. You are your own accuser. God knows the accusations, and you are really bound to try and be honest. Are we always honest? No, the temptation to be self-righteous and to see ourselves as right is too strong. But, it's a wonderful custom or habit

There isn't any other place in our lives where we do this. Where have I gone wrong during the past week? And then, once you admit that, *what am I going to do about it?* Most of it is little stuff, but we must look at the big and the little.

Here's a scenario: *When my spouse (or boss, friend, or child) yells at me, I almost go berserk. It's almost all that I can do to keep from throwing something at the wall or wanting to push him/her and make him/her shut up. But wait a minute—I felt that way twice last week. I've got to figure out how to avoid getting to that place. How can I make next week better? How can I get rid of that?*

That's the advantage of the examination of conscience. It must be active, not just a simple listing of shortcomings. Don't just run down the list and say, "Oops, but hey, I didn't do too badly. Go ahead, bless me, Father!" Take it to the next step and figure out how to prevent it from happening again. Also, reconciliation is a form of a discipline, and frankly, we could use more discipline.

Remember, each of the Sacraments involves an encounter with Jesus Christ—the historic Christ—made real and concrete in our presence by the Sacrament. When you have the Sacrament of Penance, you look at your life and examine your true sins. You admit those imperfections, and commit to trying to do better. God's grace flows into our souls, directly into us at that moment and at that point of contact. It's just as real as if Jesus had reached out and touched us on the shoulder and said, "Get up and don't do that anymore."

What happens when you have committed a grave sin and may have confessed it to God, but not been through the Sacrament of Penance with a priest? Well, we're faced with Church law, and this is one that I agree with. Because we're so prone to giving ourselves the benefit of the doubt, the Church has made a law that if you perform a grave sin, and this gift of reconciliation is present, then you have an obligation to use it. Specifically, the Church puts on us the obligation to confess all grave sins of which we are aware. Remember, though, it is not a grave sin to miss morning prayers. Remember also that the essence of reconciliation is responding to God's infinite love for us regardless of our weaknesses and blemishes.

FORGIVENESS

"How can you tell when an Irishman has dementia? He forgets every-thing but the grudges!"

—Urban legend

To a great extent, forgiveness is what the church is all about. Forgiveness is all about the relationship between the human family and almighty God. The reality of forgiveness is the reason and cause that brought God into the human story in the person of Jesus of Nazareth.

Why is forgiveness so important? Because each and every one of us is a frail human being. We share life with others. We have a relationship with God. In sharing that life and in relating to God, we experience many bumps along the road. We ALL sin! *We ALL Sin!*

If sin were the only reality in our lives, this experience on earth would be devastatingly destructive, continually depressing, and an ongoing experience of defeat and loss.

In the midst of that dark reality of sin and human failure, and the pain we inflict on each other, in the midst of all these disappointments, nevertheless a beautiful light of joy shines. That light and the subsequent joy come from the reality of forgiveness. The greatest sin in the human story is that we turn away from God and reject the infinite love that He showers upon us. That is THE sin. It is the sin of Adam and Eve. It is the sin of Cain and Abel. That is the sin of Noah and his sons. Those stories in the first few chapters of the Bible are not cute fairy tales. They represent the sacred authors' efforts to convey to God's people that sin has been part of our story from the first point of our existence, and it continues today.

Despite the universal presence of sin in our lives, we are nevertheless a redeemed people lifted out of our sin and to our heavenly Father through the saving actions of Jesus Christ. By His presence among us, His teaching, His example and by entering into His life via the sacraments, our frail natures are joined to an infinitely loving God, and in a very limited sense we come to share in His life.

All of that is obviously true in a theological sense. But what does that mean to each of us in our day-to-day lives? It means every single one of us need to be clearly conscious of three things: God's love for them individually, their redemption, and the need to mirror God's forgiveness with those with whom they are sharing life.

We've all been hurt. You can't live in a family, neighborhood, office, plant, home, or political organization without rubbing up against men and women who differ with you. Not all of those neighbors of ours have earned their doctorate in diplomacy! When we're tired, irritable, defensive, or frightened, our defenses go into action and we frequently find ourselves striking out, not only hurting people, but also much worse—*having an actual desire to inflict pain.*

I'm talking about minor infractions and conflicts in which all of us find ourselves. What should we do? When we kneel in the back of the Church to prepare ourselves for the sacrament of penance, we don't have to spend a lot of time on the number of murders or incidents of adultery or embezzlement of which we have been involved. The range of sins is very narrow. Most of us, frankly, are third-class sinners (meaning we don't commit the major sins.) I do not wish to downplay the reality of widespread moral failure in our lives, but the fact is that most of us live fairly structured lives on our jobs and in our families, and those structures help us to be morally good most of the time.

So, when one of us is examining our conscience, we can skip rapidly over six of the commandments, and go to where most of us fail with some frequency: the first three commandments, which deal with our relationship with God, and the seventh, ninth, and tenth. In other words, we do not give the worship of God the attention in our lives that it calls for. This is the area where the average person really needs to develop a more sensitive conscience.

How many people have you seen crying despondently in the past year? My guess is that if you have, it wasn't because of a cancer diagnosis or an automobile accident. The greatest source of pain that we cause to those around us comes from our lack of charity, our inordinate criticism, and our inability to offer appropriate appreciation. When we do these cruel things with any degree of consciousness, they are sinful.

I doubt very seriously that there is any parish where there are not a number of families or individuals who refuse to talk to other people within the same parish. They come down the center aisle together to receive their Eucharistic Lord, and they are one with Christ. However, when they pass in the parking lot, nothing is exchanged but glares. This really is a moral and spiritual tragedy! The sinfulness that I'm referring to here is not grave, it is not a mortal sin; but these actions are the conscious inflicting of pain, and the participants are passing up the opportunity for letting the love and forgiveness of Jesus pass through them to the lives of their neighbors and friends. When we are preparing for the examination of conscience, we should really concentrate on this.

Why do we hold grudges? Sad to say, it's because the person holding that grudge derives a certain amount of morose pleasure out of it. They have put that person who has offended them in a special category—they've decided that this is a person who needs not be respected nor appreciated, and if we have the opportunity, we should try to get back at them.

For a person trying to follow Christ, holding grudges is a real moral cancer. It not only brings pain to the recipient of the grudge, but it can cause decay in the day-to-day life of the person holding that grudge.

Fighting and conflict, bitterness and misunderstandings are very frequent causes of pain and suffering in our lives, but God has put a sweetener into our sinful souls! When we forgive, when we forget, when we let the grudge go, there is a rush of relaxing joy in our emotions and in our stomachs that is really a wonderful natural gift. Let's constantly be working to receive that gift.

In the presence of the Blessed Sacrament, we confront ourselves with our tendency toward bitterness, negativism, hypercriticism, or lack of appreciation, and we need to connect it with the Eucharist. We need to relate it to the fact that on Sunday morning we receive into our lives nothing less than the forgiving presence of Jesus. When we say the Rosary or the

Our Father at home or at Mass, we ask God to *forgive us the way we forgive other people!* If we don't really mean that, it's a lie. Not that we shouldn't say the Lord's Prayer, but when we say the Lord's Prayer, we should say it and be conscious of the fact that we are entering into a contract with God about forgiveness. He has forgiven us. All He requires is sorrow. We are forgiven not when we receive the sacrament of penance, but the instant we are sorry for being wrong. At that very instant, He forgives us! Should we not do the same with others? Can we really claim to be a follower of Jesus when we remember that four years ago a certain person snubbed us at the altar society meeting?

This is really an important goal for Catholics who want to imitate the life of Jesus Christ. We want to be able to say with St. Paul, "I live now, not I, but Christ lives in me. For me to live IS Christ."

Frequently people say, "I don't have any reason to go to the sacrament of penance; I'm living a good life." That is wonderful, and something for which a person should thank God! But, is he or she really saying that they are devoid of pettiness, cruelty, and backbiting? For most of us, that is not true.

Walking in the footsteps of Jesus is not easy. Most of us don't think about it very much, but if the subject comes up, we pay lip service to it, because, well, hey, we are faithful in our marriage and haven't committed any major crimes. How many of us can say, "I almost never criticize others unfairly. I try never to be guilty of rash judgment. I'm always respectful of others." Those people are indeed blessed, but the rest of us have more work to do.

COMMUNION OF SAINTS

"A great prayer for life is urgently needed, a prayer which will rise up throughout the world. Let us pray an impassioned plea to our God on behalf of life!"
—*Bishop John McCarthy, in a Pastoral Letter on Respect for Life*

Do you ever give much thought to why cereal and shoe companies spend so much money hiring famous people to advertise their products? It's amazing. They pay so little to the laborers in the countries where they actually do the production, yet spend a sizable amount of their budget to pay celebrities to advertise the product. Why is that? The businessmen who are marketing these products are (obviously) there to make money. They know that there is an innate tendency in most human beings to slip rather easily into hero worship. By that, I mean we look and see other people, who we don't know personally, but we know about, who have accomplished great things. For example, in golf, Tiger Woods, or in biking, Lance Armstrong. These men are now somewhat fallen heroes, but their stories genuinely inspired many others and their faces sold a million products before they fell. We like hero worship. It's human nature.

The Church has many weaknesses—structured weaknesses—but it also has many gifts. One of the gifts is that it seems to have almost an innate ability to adapt its programs around human nature. If people want to move in a certain direction, if they want to be good, and be more like Jesus Christ, then they want to act in a certain way. However, they often feel they are out there by themselves—so it's a great help for the average human being if you *place in front of them an example of someone who was heroically good, awesomely generous, totally committed to Jesus, and willing to serve Him no matter what the cost.* Out of this comes the practice of the Church to highly respect men and women who have lived extraordinary lives of goodness. Our name for these wonderful heroes is "saints." I think the Church has made a mistake in deciding to formalize canonization, which is the process of designating sainthood. In my opinion, a better system was in place for the first 1,000 years.

When the general population decided that someone was a saint, what did that mean? Just that they are venerable. We ought to respect them. We ought to imitate them. Mother Theresa would have rightly been considered a saint. Centuries ago, the Church decided to formalize the process, and when some group wanted to have a person recognized as a saint, they applied for canonization. This is usually done by religious orders that are endeavoring to get their founder or one of their most important members recognized for sanctity.

It almost seems now that we've made it some sort of passport to eternal life, or a document that verifies they actually got into Heaven. I believe that the Church should not have done that.

Part of the rationalization for the formal process is that the Church is worried about "phonies." For example, there was a woman, Theresa Neumann, in Germany, with famous stigmata, before the Second World War. She did have stigmata, but it may have been psychologically induced. In order to protect the faithful, the Church has overcompensated, trying to completely control it.

I get amused when people talk about Catholics "worshipping" the saints. If your daughter were seriously ill, would you ask your living mother to pray for her recovery? Of course you would. Would you ask your grandmother, who's deceased, but knows what's going on down here, to pray for her? Why not? If people think that someone is wonderfully holy, they pray to them. I pray to my family. I think my parents and grandparents are with God. When I've got troubles, I tell them to get on the stick and pray. What are they doing up there? Don't leave me down here without help. I'm being a bit facetious, of course, but that's one way I explain the Communion of Saints.

Let's take a positive view of the human tendency towards imitating heroes. It's a wonderful thing if the hero or model is a good person- a generous person- a faithful person. When other people try to imitate this person, *they generate goodness into the next generation.* Ultimately, we must make our own decisions. We need to give all we have to become the best we can be. Our models, our heroes and heroines, cannot transform us. They can, however, give us a little extra motivation to move ourselves along in the right direction.

THE ROSARY

"A great prayer for life is urgently needed, a prayer which will rise up throughout the world. Let us pray an impassioned plea to our God on behalf of life!"
—*Bishop John McCarthy, in a Pastoral Letter on Respect for Life*

One of the three principle activities inside the life of the Church is prayer and worship. Prayer manifests itself in many different ways.

The most important single manifestation of prayer in the Catholic Church is the celebration of the Eucharist. We call this the Mass. Besides the Mass, there are countless methods of prayer: mental prayer, centering prayer, verbal prayer, community prayer, and individual prayer. These are all forms of prayer. However, after the Mass, the most popular single prayer in the West is the Rosary.

The Rosary is a prayer that seems extraordinarily dull if people don't understand it. We've taken two prayers out of the Bible—the Lord's Prayer (Our Father) and the Hail Mary (half of which is in the Bible)—and we put them together into a strange form. The story of how it began is very interesting.

In medieval times during the monastic movement, the monasteries were very powerful. There were monasteries all over Europe. The primary activity of the monks was prayer. They also made wine, grew food, and built their own schools, but they truly centered their life on prayer. They took their office—oficium, which means duty, burden, or responsibility—seriously, and their office was the office of prayer. They prayed all day long. They got up around 3:00am or 4:00am to say a prayer called "matins." Then came "prime" at dawn, "terce (third hour)" at 9am, "sext (sixth hour)" at noon and "none", around nine after sunset, and finally compline, or night prayer.

The monks would stop what they were doing and go to the chapel to pray at all these times if they could. They'd all pray together. The shepherds, the uneducated brothers that belonged to the monastery, could not read. They didn't know any Latin, but they did know the Our Father and they'd learned the Hail Mary. So, one or more of the monks got the idea of saying an Our Father and ten Hail Mary's, and then you'd close that out with the Gloria, which is an ending prayer. "Glory be to the Father, and to the Son, and to the Holy Spirit. As it was in the beginning, is now and ever shall be, world without end. Amen." That ends a single decade (section of the Rosary).

The rosaries of the really pious people consisted of fifteen decades. They had built up the idea of meditating on the life of Jesus, and this is what they wanted the simple people to do. There are joyful mysteries, sorrowful mysteries, and glorious mysteries (although the word mystery is misused here- several are actually historical events). It's "mysterious" in the broad sense of some strange occurrence of God's action in our lives.

In this manner, the first set of ten prayers (called a decade) allows you to reflect on how Jesus's birth story got started with the annunciation. The angel comes to Mary and says, "You are pregnant!" Then Mary goes off to visit Elizabeth—the second joyous mystery. Then there is the birth of Jesus, then the presentation at the temple, and finally finding the adolescent Jesus at the temple. This is followed by the sorrowful mysteries and the glorious mysteries.

So one way to look at the Rosary is that it is lovely background music—a way to focus our thoughts as we pray. That's the Rosary in its ideal manifestation. The life of Jesus Christ is laid out in three major segments: joyous, sorrowful, and glorious.

Also, note that there are one hundred and fifty Hail Mary's in a full Rosary. There are also one hundred and fifty psalms. So, while the monks inside were saying their office, their "oficium," reading the Psalms from the Old Testament, the poor peasant on the other side of the wall was just saying Hail Mary's for each one of those. There is a parallel structure between the chanting of the office in the great cathedrals inside and the simple peasant saying the hundred and fifty Hail Mary's outside, while he is meditating on the life and actions of Jesus Christ.

The Rosary offers us a simple, humble prayer. In most difficult situations, we're not in control, and it's a really nice prayer to say to gain a sense of control. I personally don't use the Rosary as my preferential form of daily prayer. However, especially when I am scared or worried, I find myself saying almost instinctively saying this beautiful prayer. For example, a few months ago I was stuck in an MRI getting a scan for over two hours. Let me tell you, I started praying the Rosary. This devotion kept me focused and sane.

The Rosary ties us in with the last fifteen hundred years. There's a sense of security in thinking of St. Augustine in the fifth century saying the Rosary, and St. Thomas Aquinas in the twelfth century, and Benedict in the seventeenth saying the Rosary. I like that idea—that it is a unifying prayer. When you consider the billions of people over the centuries that have prayed the Rosary, you realize how much this prayer bonds us.

The best thing about going to a Papal audience is watching the unity of the Church in prayer. Everybody still knows some Latin hymns. We can come together from all over the world, and unite together in prayer. To hear fifty or a hundred thousand people singing together is terrific! It literally sends chills up and down my spine.

Devotion is a word that is used to cover the many different forms of prayer that reflect our various approaches to God within the Church. The Stations of the Cross, the Nine First Fridays, and the Devotion to the Sacred Heart are all forms of devotions. The Rosary, however, is the single most popular form of devotion in the life of the Church. This form of prayer is being utilized in South Africa, the Ukraine and Japan even as we sit here.

Hail Mary, Full of Grace, the Lord is with Thee!
Blessed art thou amongst women,
And blessed is the fruit of thy womb, Jesus.
Holy Mary, Mother of God,
Pray for us sinners,
Now, and at the hour of our death.

Amen

THE SACRAMENTS:
A COMMUNITY EXPERIENCE

"I have heard some among us boast that they have taken a strong position in "protecting the Sacraments" from those judged "not worthy" enough to celebrate these fundamental experiences of the Catholic Faith. This attitude is quite different from the attitude of the Good Shepherd who searches for the stray and cares for them."
—*Bishop John McCarthy*

Most Catholics look back on their own spiritual journeys and can remember certain moments in time that were very special to them. Usually, these memories are built around the sacraments. People have a baptismal certificate to remind them of the day that they were baptized into the Church. They remember their First Holy Communion class, when they were all dressed in white. Many remember the day of their Confirmation and the man with the funny hat who came out to administer the Sacrament. Later on, people will look back and remember the very special day of their marriage. Also, in rare cases these days, people remember when a man is ordained to the priesthood, and he takes the Holy Orders. While we don't remember our deaths, our friends and relatives do, and they mark that day with care and gentle memories.

I think I can safely say for most of us, these special sacramental events, while being extraordinarily personal, are seen also as very individualistic. I believe this is a mistake. Among the many changes of the second Vatican council was the effort by liturgists, theologians, and others in leadership positions to sensitize us to the idea that while there is always an extremely important individual component in the reception of a sacrament, the *communal portion of the sacrament actually outweighs the individualistic aspects.*

Let's walk through the sacraments reflecting on this concept:

We begin, of course, with **Baptism**. When a baby is born, he arrives and is welcomed as a member of a family. The mother and father provide (I'm talking about the ideal, here) an environment for the child to live and grow to maturity. That's natural birth. When those same parents and god-parents take that child to the Church and see him washed with the holy waters of Baptism, that child enters into the universal religious family that is the Church.

I regret that so many parents see Baptism as a quaint little *private* cer-emony. They get pictures of beautiful little Maria in her white dress with the godfather holding the lit candle, and then it's home to the reception where the family and friends will celebrate the baby's baptism and toast the parents. There is nothing wrong with that, but if they don't see that the big event is not the baptism of the baby into this family, but its entry into the universal church and the establishment of a relationship with Jesus, which is eternal, then sadly, something very important is missing.

This communal aspect is not unique to Baptism, but actually perme-ates all of the sacraments. One of my favorite liturgical changes from the second Vatican council applies to the next Sacrament: the Eucharistic pro-cession at Mass. There are still a few people out there who remember the Church before the council. Remember the communion railing, where we knelt and received Eucharist individually? Our individuality was symbol-ized by our being alone at the Communion railing. The procession con-veys the opposite mood. We're on a journey; we are walking together and traveling together, being nourished by the bread of life together! This is a wonderful image right out of both the Old and the New Testaments.

Perhaps someone might think that there is no communal aspect to the sacrament of **Penance.** They couldn't be more wrong. Penance began in the early Church *only* as a communal event. The early Christians saw that when they turned their back on Jesus of Nazareth, when they capitulated in the face of persecution to idolatry, they were failing the Church. When they came to the church to do penance, they stood before the community and apologized for their failures. The Church believed then, as it does now, that we are forgiven the instant that we are sorry as far as God is concerned, but we still have a responsibility to lessen the harm done to the community. Just as all politics are local, all sin is social!

Confirmation is a salute to the fact that this young person has matured enough to assume some responsibility for his or her membership in the Church. There is a price tag to being a follower of Jesus. Responsibilities are present. At Confirmation, the young person being confirmed, in a very visible and vocal manner, accepts those responsibilities with pride and generosity.

The communal implications of **Marriage** and **Holy Orders** are likewise, very obvious. When that young man and that young woman vow themselves to each other, the world becomes a different place. We have now not merely two individuals, but a family. This family is actually a tiny church with the same responsibilities that the universal Church has as well. Those responsibilities simply must be lived out in the context of this particular home.

What about the **Last Rights, now known as the Anointing** of the Sick? Surely, there is nothing more individualistic than death! Even with death, the Church sees this event as a beautiful pulling together of the totality of Christian life. A child is born, baptized, nourished by the Eucharist, absolved from sin, entered into marriage or holy orders, and now the Church will celebrate that life and the prayer of the Church will envelop the dying person. When death itself comes, the Church will raise that deceased person towards God, give thanks for the life that has ended, and offer prayers for an eternal life of joy.

The sacraments are *COMMUNAL* events, and if we see them in this light, we lose nothing in terms of their individual aspects, but gain from this view a far deeper, more profound understanding of what Christian living is all about! We are not alone. We are united with Jesus, and through Jesus we are united with everyone else who shares our faith.

HEAVEN

"We may be surprised at the people we find in heaven.
God has a soft spot for sinners."
— *Desmond Tutu*

I try to live my life centered on my firm and total belief (note that I use the word belief) that human life continues after the experience of death on this planet. I have very strong feelings about it, but I must stress again that my belief in the afterlife is a *belief.* It's something I have faith in. It's something I'm committed to. It's something that I pray with all my heart is true and real, but I don't have proof of it. In trying to live my life day by day in a way that would not jeopardize what I think is my potential for eternal life, I encounter a certain amount of difficulties, and by my selfish standards, even hardships.   *What if it is not true?* Well, if it's not true, there won't be anything, and I won't have anything to worry about! If it is true, then living a good life will be rewarded, and it was a very smart move on my part.

The vast, vast majority of the human race has embraced the concept that human life continues beyond death. Whether we're talking about Neolithic man, or the Egyptians or the Greeks or the Africans today living south of the Sahara, or even the people who live in midtown Manhattan, the vast majority of people are committed to a belief in the afterlife. Quite frankly, one of the reasons that we believe in eternal life is the fact that we realize that virtually everyone else does, too, and that gives us a psychological reason for accepting that concept (since it's been so universally held throughout history.) It's important to note that, again, we are talking about faith, not proven fact.

Some cynics, of course, who reject the idea of the continuation of some form of life following physical death, pooh-pooh the idea and cite the fact that there is no scientific proof of anyone ever returning from the grave to give us a report. (Of course, that is only true with one notable exception!) I'm aware of the countless people who have had near-death experiences and report a great sense of peacefulness and comfort, and when they were being resuscitated, were resistant because they liked what they saw and where they were going. However, none of these people were actually declared dead. If and when they were declared dead, they did not return to tell us about it.

Those are the facts. Most people believe that we are created for eternal life. They believe that it's important to live good lives in order to be happy in the eternal future that awaits them.

I'm going to limit myself just to the Roman Catholic position on possible post-death developments. There are only three: one is temporary, and two are permanent.

Jesus of Nazareth frequently talked about the need to live a good life, to walk in His footsteps, and place our faith in Him and be united with Him by joining in His death and resurrection. The Church has taken those many statements about a coming judgment and built a rather complex moral theology around them, which accents the thesis that a life of eternal joy is dependent upon a generous and faithful life here on earth. That eternal joy is what we call Heaven. If I told you everything that I know about Heaven, I would not need more than two more sentences. Essentially, we see it as an intimate personal union with God, who has to an infinite degree every good quality that our human brains could conjure up. However, quite frankly, my own limited brain cannot grasp infinite joy, infinite wisdom, infinite power, or the even the word "infinite" by itself! I know what I mean, but I cannot get my brain around it.

Personally, I like to believe that the vast majority of the human race will live eternally with God. If that is not true, the salvific mission of Jesus was less than successful.

The other possibility is Hell. This is easier to handle. Over the centuries, people have described Hell as a place of everlasting torment, but theologically speaking, the basic definition is eternal separation from God, who is the cause of our existence. Therefore, Hell would be eternal frustration and disappointment.

Pope John Paul II startled a lot of people a few years ago when he stated in a very public manner that the fire in Hell is strictly metaphorical language. He stressed again that Hell is essentially separation from the reason for our existence. I personally don't think that Hell is a very crowded place.

And then, there's purgatory. This is not as clear in our teaching as the first two possibilities, Heaven and Hell, and is essentially a development of Roman Catholic moral theology. The theologians recognized that people were capable of serious failures in their moral conduct, and since God is a just God, somehow people should atone for their moral blemishes. Thus "Purgatory" entered into the Roman Catholic language. There is only one place in sacred scripture where there is a vague mention of a concept of purgatory, which is when the great Jewish man, Judas Maccabeus, said that it was a holy and pious thought to pray for the dead that they may be released from their sins. That book, Maccabees, is among those books rejected by the Protestants, primarily because of that very statement!

So where are we with purgatory? It's all well and good to wrestle with our potential destiny, but it's more important to deal with ourselves in the here and now. Our nature tells us that we are instinctively called to be good, to use our natural gifts, to be generous, and to use those gifts on behalf of others. Live a good life, confident of the infinite goodness of God, and don't worry!

So what do I think will happen after I take my last breath here on earth? Well, heck, I don't know! BUT, I believe in an infinitely just, infinitely loving and forgiving God. Like most of us, I will have a lot to account for in terms of mistakes, but I'm not afraid, because I believe that when my heart stops and the doctor officially says "he's gone," John McCarthy will not only be NOT gone, but he will be *there, with God forever and ever*. AND with all the people that he likes. Of course, there will also be all those people that he dislikes, too...

From my frame of reference, it's a waste of time to sit around wondering what Heaven will be like. Look around: everything that we see today—life, light, beauty, birds, sky, working cars, ice water—all of these things are wonderful, and you and I are going to have all that and infinitely more, *forever, forever, and forever!* And yet, as a human being, I've got to back off of that time frame, because it begins to sound boring. But in heaven, there is no time, no tomorrow, no change in the weather, no change, period. There is no sense of time in eternity, which is tough to grasp.

If pressed (repeated and incessantly by my editor) to describe what I imagine heaven to look like in earthly terms, however, then here is my personal vision. I would weigh exactly 178 lbs. I'd be 45 years old, and would have gotten rid of all of my enemies. I'd be surrounded by dear, close friends who love discussing politics, and although there would be lots of political conflicts, we would win them all. I would get to drink Scotch with good friends and enjoy their company. But I must say again, all of this vision is simply degrading to the true concept of heaven! Does that reduce Heaven to being a wonderful picnic? No, that is just the best thing our limited human brains can imagine. It's going to be better—yes—*infinitely* better than that!

HELL

*"The images of hell that Sacred Scripture presents to us must be
correctly interpreted. They show the complete frustration and
emptiness of life without God. <u>Rather</u> than a place, hell indicates
the state of those who freely and definitively separate themselves from
God, the source of all life and joy."*
—*Pope John Paul II (at the General Audience on July 28, 1999)*

I have no problem with the Church's teachings on Hell. Jesus, in His public life, made references to loss of the eternal soul. The Church formally
teaches that there is such a place, such a possible relationship. We believe
that the soul is created for eternity, so I've got to take the issue of Hell very,
very seriously.

The question is—who's there? Who occupies Hell? Some fundamentalist Protestants, who believe that baptism is absolutely essential for salvation, believe that the vast majority of the human population from all
time is going to spend all of eternity in Hell. I certainly don't accept that!
I don't believe in that at all. We have a gentle way around that: "baptism
of desire." The fundamentalist Protestants and the Roman Catholics do
agree on the importance of both faith in Jesus Christ and baptism, but the
Catholic Church has a gentler frame of reference, which is that if a person
wants to do what's right, wants to do good, wants to do whatever Yahweh,
or the Great Spirit of the Native Americans, directs, we call that a "baptism of desire." That's a good person, and that person achieves salvation on
innate goodness.

What about terrible sins? This is when it gets sloppy. You have to
decide what you think Hell is. My understanding of the official position

of the Roman Catholic Church is that Hell is the total permanent, eternal separation from your purpose, which is GOD. Therefore, that would be tremendously maddening. Even John Paul II, in his last pontificate, said that the phrase "the flames of hell" is rhetoric. There's nothing to burn. This is not going to please people who like nice, even, black and white concepts.

The essence of our faith is relationships. The principle relationship is with God.

Psychologically, it doesn't start off that way, but ultimately, theologically, it is with God. The second relationship is with ourselves, and then, third, with those with whom we share life. If we cannot have that relationship with God, which we think brings infinite joy and everlasting happiness, we will be in Hell. Whether or not that involves pain, I don't know.

But I doubt it. I think it's more like frustration. But, is it frustration at a level that people can handle and live with forever? I don't know.

I said I don't have any problems with the Catholic Church's teachings on Hell, but that's partly because the teachings are very vague. The Church claims to know people who are in Heaven, when it canonizes people. It never, ever claims to know that someone is damned for all eternity.

Part of our problem with Hell is that in times past, we knew nothing of human nature or psychology—what human freedom is—and we judged people very harshly. We certainly know that we have free will, but we have only recently begun to realize the extraordinary complexities (especially including the intricate chemistries within our brains) that affect our decisions, emotions and judgments. Knowing all these complexities and nuances that go into human decisions will help us better understand human nature (as well as mental illness.).

Imagine saying that if you deliberately ate meat on Friday, it was a grave sin. Or if you deliberately and carelessly failed to go to Mass on Sunday, that was a grave sin. The Church said it was! But, please note, it wouldn't say that today. I can conceive that a rebellion against the Church could be grave, but a grave sin is not eating a cheeseburger or sleeping late on Sunday. We do, of course, have an obligation to worship God, and we should be guided by the Church in this regard. Happily, the Church today is much more sensitive regarding the complexities that are present in human judgment.

I do believe the awesome powers that human beings have to think and love and choose from their souls carries responsibility. I do think that in living our lives on this planet for thirty, sixty, or ninety years, we are expected to utilize the gifts that we have and fulfill the responsibilities that we've been handed. How God sorts this out, I don't know. I have to tell you quite frankly that I am happy to leave that up to Him. I have a belief in an infinite, just God, an infinite loving God, and I think everything's going to turn out all right.

PAPAL INFALLIBILITY

"I believe that the Church is infallible but I don't think that infallibility—that gift that God will guide it in moments of crisis—was completely lodged in one human head. It is the Community of Faith, the Church, that is guided by the Holy Spirit so that it is always faithful to the essential message of Jesus of Nazareth."
—Bishop John McCarthy

The Church's teaching that the Pope—the Bishop of Rome and successor of St. Peter—enjoys papal infallibility is one of the most controversial aspects of the Catholic Church in the modern world, most especially in its relationship to other religions. A clear understanding of this teaching began in 1870, when the first Vatican council defined it. The Council said that the Bishop of Rome, *when he is exercising his authority as Bishop of the Universal Church, and he teaches something about Catholic doctrine with the intention of binding across the world,* that teaching is infallible.

That definition, if properly understood, has many boundaries and constraints on it. Nevertheless, a very common misunderstanding is that the Pope himself does not sin, and that anything he chooses to do is all right. That would be an obvious farce, and let's not waste time on it! Jesus and His Mother are without sin, but the rest of us are not exempt.

Let me repeat: to be "infallible," the Pope would have to be teaching in a formal manner, exercising his jurisdiction as Bishop of the Universal Church, with the teaching limited to doctrine. The Pope's view on economics, sociology, or gender, etc., would have no more infallibility than the next person.

While everyone knows about the teaching of infallibility, not everyone is conscious that a second aspect of this teaching is that the Pope, as Universal Shepherd, *enjoys immediate and universal jurisdiction over every aspect of the Church*. What does this mean? Well, it means that the Pope can tell me in Austin, Texas, that I cannot sign a hospital contract with the Daughters of Charity. He has direct domain over material resources across the globe.

The concept of papal infallibility by itself is too much for most other Christian denominations. If they really understood the implications of immediate and universal jurisdiction, I believe they would have greater issues with it than the better-known notion of papal infallibility.

Let me make something perfectly clear. The papacy has always been an extraordinary force in the life of the Church, developing over 2000 years. Those who hold for papal infallibility claim that this concept is present from the life of the infant Church. Those who oppose it would say that it is a factor that has come forth gradually in the unfolding of history.

Let's go back to the first century. There are many reasons for biblical scholars to assert that Peter was the leader of the apostles. All four gospels mentioned the apostles by name, and all four of them have different arrangements of the names, except that all four put Peter's name first. There is a text: "Whom do you say that I am? Thou are the Son of the Living God. Blessed are thou, Simon bar Jonah, for flesh and blood has not revealed this to you but my Father in Heaven." This text and others like it reflects Peter's unique position.

Over the next 200 or 300 years, there was a gradual increase in the recognition of the importance of the Bishop of Rome. More and more secular authorities recognized that man as the leader of the Church. By the time of Constantine in the beginning of the 4th century, it was clearly understood that the Bishop of Rome was the most important Prelate in the Church. By the 6th and 7th centuries, the Pope was exercising the power to appoint bishops in other parts of the world (whereas in earlier centuries, bishops were chosen within the local church by the members of that church). By the 10th century, the papacy was organized very much as it is today, with the Pope sending legates to different parts of the world to represent him on important issues. However, the role of the papacy became very clear during the Protestant reformation, when the church began to look to the Bishop of Rome to be the chief defender of the church in that period of crisis.

Throughout all of this period, there was great deference shown to the papacy. The Pope had administrative powers that he exercised. The Bishop of Rome was pre-eminent above any other Bishop in the universal church, *but it was never defined that he was infallible.*

For that, we look to Rome in 1870, when the first Vatican Council convened. That council was called and played out under a cloud. Pope Pius IX had just been stripped of the territory in central Italy, which he governed not just in religious matters, but in civic, economic, and social matters as well. This territory was called the Papal States, and had been independent of other political leaders since the 8th century. There are many authors who think that Pope Pius IX brought forth the issue of papal infallibility as some sort of a fallback position for the loss of his prestige, and his political and economic independence. There are arguments on both sides.

We do know that the Council was convened in an extraordinarily hectic time in Europe. Prussia and other German principalities were at war with France. An Italian revolutionary, Garibaldi, was in the process of unifying Italy, and his forces occupied Rome. This caused many bishops to leave the Council early. Others left early simply because they did not want to vote on the subject. Pope Pious IX aggressively pursued the vote on infallibility. Out of the hundreds of bishops who had attended the Council, many were not present to vote. Of those that voted, two bishops alone voted against infallibility, Interestingly, one was from Little Rock, Arkansas. The joke was that the little rock took on the big rock!

Where are we today? If you challenge a defined teaching, you slightly separate yourself from the Church. You cannot be a cafeteria Catholic, where you pick and choose which pieces of the Church's teachings you would like. Pope John Paul II admitted very frankly that he understood that the Church's doctrine of infallibility was one of the greatest obstacles to Christian unity in the 21st century. In fact, although he said that he could not give it up, he wanted to be advised on how to use it more effectively.

Practicing Catholics are not free to deny papal infallibility without risking a rupture between themselves and the Universal Church. The vast majority of Catholics really never think about it, but it is a very heavy problem confronting anyone with a strong desire to bring about the unity of Christians across the world—- a unity which is so desperately needed in this century, as Christians are becoming an ever-smaller minority on the planet.

Most Catholics correctly concentrate their faith in the person of Jesus of Nazareth. They know that He is their Savior, and the Savior of Humanity. Life within the Church brings enormous blessings, but often also brings complications that produce tension and frustration. We must lessen our concern about those distractions, and recommit ourselves ever more to Jesus Christ.

THE PRIESTHOOD

*"We have invested priests, especially for the last thousand years, with
great importance at the organizational core of the Catholic church. We
treat a priest as though he is very special. And he really isn't, except as
a servant. A priest is simply a servant."*
—Bishop John McCarthy

Today the Roman Catholic priesthood is under a magnifying glass.
Catholics, as a group, are often fascinated by the priesthood. Those that
don't share the Catholic faith are mystified, confused, and frequently hostile to the idea of the priesthood. Let's talk about the Catholics first.

First of all, the priesthood is the organizational core of the Roman
Catholic Church. The Roman Catholic Church is the largest voluntary
organization on earth, present in almost every country in the world, and
possessing one billion, two hundred million members. Of course, the
Roman Catholic Church has strong dotted-line relationships with other
churches, most especially the Orthodox, but also with Lutherans and
Anglicans. Given that fact, the Catholic priesthood ought to be drawing large numbers of people into its ranks, because this group is such a
vital part of an enormous organization. But in point of fact, *the number
of men seeking ordination has been dropping dramatically for almost fifty
years.*

Take a look at these figures: In 1962, there were 42 million Roman
Catholics in the United States served by 55,000 priests. Forty years later, in
2002, the number of Catholics in the United States had swelled to 65 million, and the number of priests had fallen to 37,000. This translates into a
disaster. Any thoughtful observer needs to ask "Why? Why is this central

organizational core of the largest voluntary organization on earth having such trouble developing new leaders, without whom the Church will not be able to function?"

There are many reasons for this decline. Sadly, in the last couple of decades, there have been highly publicized, tragic cases of priestly pedophilia, and the terrible actions of these relatively few men have greatly tarnished the overall reputation of the priesthood. Subsequent cover-ups by Church leaders have been nothing short of disastrous. Any thoughtful leader should know that efforts to cover up a problem or a scandal almost invariably produce a bigger problem than the original offense. On a more positive note, in 2012, the Vatican held a symposium to confront and eliminate the "deadly culture of silence" that surrounded the agonizing scandal of child abuse by clergy. I applaud the Holy See for his willingness to publicly address this painful issue that flows out of a long established, very wrong and ultimately useless effort to protect the Church's reputation in the face of scandalous abuse. When evil is done it must consistently be confronted and exposed, and our Church leaders must go above and beyond to ensure that the protection of the victims is always prioritized over the reputation of the Church.

Another significant reason for the decline in vocations is the fact that until the recent past, women were the greatest source of encouragement within the Roman Catholic Church to young men considering the priesthood. Catholic mothers, whether you were talking about Ireland, or Germany, or Brazil, or the United States, took great pride if one or several of their young boys would aspire to being ordained to the Catholic priesthood.

Over the centuries, we don't seem to see any examples of women being insulted, infuriated, offended, or hostile to the Church simply because they could not be ordained. Since the second half of the twentieth century, though, it's been a whole new ball game. With the arrival of the women's liberation movement, women became conscious of the fact that they were being discriminated against. Instead of saying "that's the way things are," they began to say, "That's not right. Why can my son become a priest but my daughter cannot?" This produced a negative reaction among Catholic women, especially in the United States and Western Europe. Now, large numbers of women not only don't encourage their sons to consider the priesthood, they actively discourage it.

There are certainly other reasons for the decrease in men seeking the priesthood as a vocation. The world itself has completely changed its approach to sexuality. Not only is the priesthood in the Catholic Church restricted to males, but it's restricted to males who are willing to take vows to live a celibate life. This was looked upon with respect until the sexual revolution hit us around fifty years ago. Instead of an eighteen-year-old boy's family reacting with adulation, praise, joy, and encouragement, honor and pride when they hear that he is going to the seminary in September, the opposite frequently occurs. They say, "He must be crazy. Why is he doing that?"

So, you've got these two revolutions—women's lib and the sexual revolution—that had tremendous impact on the number of men aspiring to the priesthood.

The facts are that at this point in time, this enormous growing Church finds itself very short-handed. A critical point here is that it's not just the numbers- it's the quality. If you have a thousand applicants for a particular job, you'll check them out very well, and find that they possess a wide range of talents. Some are geniuses, some are natural leaders, and some are clods. There are extroverts and introverts. If you're in a leadership position, and you're reviewing the next generation of leaders, you've got a broad range to choose from.

If you cut the potential applicants from a thousand to one hundred, the talent pool drops immensely. Yes, you may still get a genius, but it's less likely. If you are tremendously lucky, you may get another Ted Hesburgh, but obviously, you've lowered your odds.

The religious community, which currently runs two hundred and fifty universities in this country, cannot replace themselves as leaders of these institutions. Without exception, they've had to stop looking for clergy and go out into the lay field and choose new leaders there. This, of course, has happily opened them up to tremendous talent. So, you've got a large drop in numbers and the overwhelming contraction of the pool of potential leaders. This is why the Roman Catholic Church at this time is having such a serious problem seeing strong leaders pushed to the forefront to take over important roles and lead activities in the Church.

What is the effect of all these negative forces on those men who are already ordained? It varies. Older priests remember different times with different circumstances, and they are simply holding on until the day of their retirement. Younger priests who look ahead to the next twenty or forty years have to ask themselves, "What does it mean to be here in such an important field when it's so unattractive to other bright men in this particular age?" Does it mean there is just an inadequate vocation director? Or is that young priest conscious of the negative factors that have influenced his profession and ministry?

If he's not careful, the young priest can be discouraged. I'm happy to say that most of the younger priests that I know are doing quite well despite all the negativity swirling about them. It would be great if they could see that they were on a roll, and there were crowds pounding on the front door of the seminary trying to join the priesthood.

In one sense, however, it does have a positive impact. If you admit that the priesthood is the core of the Roman Catholic Church, and that it is crucially important, and the Church is already enormous and growing larger every day, and yet the number of priests is declining, then, each individual member of the priesthood becomes more vital, more important. That's a source of encouragement and optimism. The ideal would be if the popular view of the priesthood would change back to a more positive image. *That's what we'll pray and work towards.*

THE MOST AWESOME GIFT

"The Irish tend toward an inordinate amount of laughter.
I know—I laugh a lot. I think my desire to see humor in everything is
because when I am working, it's very often sad. For the Irish, things
were so bad for 400 years that they just had to get a laugh out
of everything they could."
—Bishop John McCarthy

God has given us many wonderful gifts. Sometimes I simply sit and gratefully reflect about things of which I am capable, or the wonderfully awesome capabilities of others that I know and share life with. So many times when we reflect on our blessings, we think of good health, close friends, adequate money. These can be gifts, and are much appreciated by those who have them. However, there are other gifts that pertain to our spiritual nature. We ought to acknowledge them, celebrate them and, perhaps most of all, we should utilize them to the maximum extent possible.

As I'm sitting here saying this, I am thinking especially of the gifts of memory and imagination. These are truly awesome. Memory allows you to relive yesterday, and the imagination enables us to plan and design what we'd hope will occur tomorrow. Great gifts!

Another gift that I consider to have tremendous importance, and be awesome in terms of its value, is the gift of humor. Mark Twain is credited for saying that "humor is mankind's greatest blessing." Perhaps he's right! Virtually everybody knows what humor is. You remember the expression that developed in a government hearing years ago where someone said, "If it walks like a duck, and quacks like a duck, it's a duck." We feel that way about humor. We recognize it.

Humor often triggers a physical response deep within us. When we laugh, we feel it not simply in the creases in our faces, but our whole bodies may shake as an instinctive reaction to good humor. But, what is it? Since no one else has defined it definitively, I'm going to take a try. I think that humor is a gift that enables us to look at one aspect of reality and correlate it instantaneously with remote ideas, people, and experiences.

When we see a person famous for pomposity and arrogance who is not aware that there is a rip on the seat of their pants, the human reaction is to instantly perceive the contrast as funny. When a great speaker, somewhat known for self-importance, makes a very wrong and contradictory statement, it is instinctive to laugh. Both of these examples are at the price of someone's feelings.

Something is said, something occurs or is seen, and instantly we connect it with another aspect of reality—but with a curve ball in it! That contrast between the objective reality and a distantly connected aspect of reality is what is hilarious. It's the contrast between the simple objective fact in front of us, and the fact that our imagination enables us to see it almost like it was a wall to be used for tennis practice. You hit it, and it bounces back. Sometimes what we think is funny, other people do not. Remember that it takes intelligence to have a great sense of humor, because people must be able to jump quickly to that distantly related possibility.

I have a brother who suffered from dementia at the end of his life, yet he always had a tremendous sense of humor. You could say something as bland as mentioning a guy walking down the street, and Frank would pop up with something to say about that which would be absolutely hilarious. The brain is filled with synapses connecting in all different directions, and people who have a great sense of humor know how to hook them up.

I was the class clown in the first grade, and I still am. I was never cruel, but we would knock down tents in a Boy Scout camp, or do other silly pranks. Mainly, I made lots of quips. I always enjoy making people laugh, and preaching from the pulpit is no exception.

One point of confusion is that people think that serious reality and humor should be separated, and yet the best balance comes from that very combination. For example, since most deaths are rather peaceful and bring about a certain amount of serenity, I would consider it a good thing at the funeral Mass to bring the congregation to see humorous aspects of the deceased person's life. (This would obviously not be true in the situation of a murder, traumatic death, or the death of a child.)

Another aspect of humor is that it can have a great leveling effect in our minds when our experience of the moment is destructive, disappointing, or even disastrous. I'm thinking of a fire that I had here in the house. I had moved out for a couple of days to have some repairs done in the house. I had nothing but a couple days' worth of clothing with me. The vicar general—of stern, farming, salt-of the earth descent—called me. It was 6:30 in the morning.

"Hello, is this Bishop McCarthy?"

"Why yes," I answered. "Good to hear your voice."

With no preamble, he blandly stated, "John, your house is on fire."

What did I do? I laughed! Why? Well, his voice portrayed no urgency, no humor, no nothing. While I can't fully express why, I've been laughing about that for over 30 years!

Why is it that humans differ so dramatically in terms of this gift? We all have the need to laugh and the potential for laughter, yet we all know individuals who rarely crack a smile, let alone share a hearty laugh. I have a tendency to separate people into two groups: one where laughter and humor is part of the fabric of their being, and the other, in which people find it frankly more difficult to be amused. What's the difference?

It would be easy to say that those prone to laughter simply have a certain type of outgoing personality, but I don't think that's a complete answer. Quite frankly, I don't know the answer, but I do know that laughter is helpful and healing. People who have the gift of humor can see life as a totality, so that although this problem is pressing today at this moment, they can still see the big picture—life, motherhood, love, Thanksgiving, newborns, and all of eternity. It balances things out!

Let's talk very briefly about the downside of humor. It's one thing to laugh at your own foibles, or at absurdity that doesn't inflect pain or destruction. It's quite another thing, however, to use humor to inflict pain or to pull others down in order that we might appear to be higher up. From a moral perspective, the gift of humor, which is ultimately from God, should never be used intentionally to inflict pain or cause sadness.

I really believe that *humor is God's gift of the ability to see reality through a lens that changes the coloration.* This man is extremely sick, but he wants to know who won the football game. That's funny, because of the contrast there between his impending death and the utter insignificance of who won the game. While not everyone standing around the man's deathbed will be amused by this, at least one person might find humor in the situation, and use that to lighten the moment. If we view life consistently through this marvelous lens of humor, we'll find that the burdens that are ours will be more easily carried, and the pain that belongs to others can be more quickly alleviated. Remember, humor is contagious. *God has given us this gift.* Let's thank Him for it and use it appropriately whenever possible.

The Church;
From Parish to Diocese and Beyond

"The Church copies a major portion of its governmental structure from that of the Roman Empire. It divides the world into provinces, and subdivides the provinces into dioceses. The Roman Empire used exactly those terms.

When one person is placed in charge, he *really* is in charge- whether that man is a pastor, a bishop or the pope. Within limits, he is the last voice on everything. Of course, each man is surrounded by consultants; he is governed by tradition and policy. He is not a freewheeling agent who can do anything he wants. When problems arise, there is the possibility of appealing over the pastor to the bishop. Likewise, one can appeal over the bishop to the pope. There is no appeal, however, over the pope."

—Bishop John McCarthy

WHERE DOES ALL THE MONEY GO?

"I believe in absolute fiscal transparency. There should be no place in the Church for any major finances that are drawn from the people that is not absolutely transparent to the people."
—*Bishop John McCarthy*

The Roman Catholic Church is perceived in the popular imagination as being an extraordinarily wealthy institution with virtually unlimited resources and the ability to do magnificent things all over the world. To a certain extent, that's true. The Church is large; it does have a lot of property; and it owns many invaluable museum pieces. (That happens when you stay around for a long time.) But in proportion to its size and its potential and its mission, the Church is not wealthy.

I have worked for the Church at every level: as pastor, as bishop, as the director of a state conference, with the national office of the United States Catholic Conference, and I've even done a certain amount of work with the Vatican. So, I've had many opportunities to look at church finances, and what I can tell you is that with great consistency, it's broke at every level. The one exception might be individual parishes, but if you asked a hundred pastors whether they had enough money, ninety-nine would say no. Ultimately, there is an inadequate amount of financial resources at every level, and as you go up to the higher levels, the resources get smaller and smaller.

The basic income of the Roman Catholic Church comes in through the local parish. That parish has the responsibility to take care of its members- meaning to worship, to teach, and to alleviate suffering. Those are the three objectives of the parish, and it has to allocate its resources as it sees fit to handle those three obligations.

The diocese has responsibilities, but it doesn't have a regular income. The diocese must turn to the parishes, either taxing 7-8% of the routine income of the parish (with the fancy name *Cathedraticum*), or asking for special financial drives and support for things like schools or other charitable programs.

The diocese possesses only a small portion of the total wealth of an area. At the national level, that only gets more dramatic. The National Conference of Catholic Bishops' building and its entire staff is constantly suffering from financial shortages, in spite of cutting back on programs and budgets. Finally, we come to the Vatican, which has virtually no income other than the kindness of the dioceses. So you see, as you go up the ladder, your claim on the basic income of the Church, which is locked in at the level of the parish, gets weaker and weaker.

Since there are so many Catholics, and the Church is so large, at each one of these levels it looks like there is great wealth. There is wealth, there is money, and there are resources, but not in relationship to the potential, and not in relationship to what the Church ought to be accomplishing at this particular point in time.

This presence of wealth gives the impression of massive resources, which the Church simply does not have. I think the most perfect examples of this are churches in Mexico. Many Americans have had the opportunity to visit Mexico, and one of the great attractions of this wonderful country is the collection of glorious churches that have been built over the last four hundred years. Many times, when you go in, you see the area above the altar lined with gold. At the same time, you see local parishioners obviously living in abject poverty. You may ask, "Why doesn't the Church use its resources to improve the standard of living?" People are truly scandalized by this.

I have several reactions to this. Number one: *the people really love that church*. This precious building was put together over hundreds of years by their hands and by the hands of their ancestors. The church is a source of beauty, joy, and encouragement, and it brings meaning to their otherwise difficult lives. The people are joined to this church by baptism, and have very strong ties to the individual church that is in their town or village.

Additionally, an elaborately decorated church does not equal a good economy. Mexico's problems are aridity and a bad economic system. The poor people are often victims of corrupt government. Taking the gold off the ceiling and over the altar and putting it in the village square is not going to change the poverty of the people, and is not going to change the economic situation. I'll give the Church good marks for speaking out constantly in Mexico and Central America, especially over the last seventy years, about the need to reform the system, the economy, to give young people a chance to get an education, and to generate an atmosphere where jobs are created. There has been extraordinarily great progress in all this in the past fifty years since I've been going back and forth to Mexico.

Another thing you hear from time to time is that the Vatican itself houses an over-the-top display of wealth that should be sold, with the profits directed to help the poor. *What do I think about that?* I completely disagree. Personally, I'm very proud of the fact that the Church has taken the trouble to put together, beyond a doubt, the best museum in the world. She has protected and guarded the cultural riches of Western Europe, and to a great extent, other parts of the world as well. Everything you see in the Vatican is primarily artistic. The Vatican is a 108-acre property that has about fifteen 400-year-old buildings on it. Today, anyone can come to the Vatican museum and see and enjoy these treasures. Speaking for myself, I would hate to see its contents sold, with priceless works of beauty and art ending up in rich people's living rooms all across the world. There's no real economy there. Yes, there is tangible wealth of gold and jewels in the Vatican museum and in St. Peter's Church, but like Mexico, that wealth cannot be directly converted to economic productivity.

God bless the Vatican, and please, take care of the museum!

WHAT'S REALLY GOING ON IN THE CHURCH?

«McCarthy says his approach…reflects his general philosophy on handling a problem: 'Deal with it aggressively, and as forcefully as you can, immediately.' He says bishops could have stemmed the sexual abuse crisis by taking that attitude and trusting lay people with the truth instead of covering up the scandal, a lesson on accountability and transparency he hopes the church will heed."
—From an interview with Eileen E. Flynn, American-Statesman Magazine, 2006

I have great love for the Catholic Church, which is why I have endeavored to give my life to its service. I appreciate the Church in so many different ways—in terms of its age; its efforts to carry on the will of our Lord and Savior, Jesus Christ; to alleviate suffering and to teach the good news of God's love for the human family—all of these things the Church does moderately well. Despite the fact that the Church is part of God's divine plan, it's also encased in a very human institution of dioceses and Bishops and parishes, and there is no human institution that doesn't carry within itself imperfections and weaknesses. That is certainly true of the Church.

One of the weaknesses of the Church in the present age (and I hope it won't last forever) is an *inordinate commitment to secrecy.* Those of us living in the modern world, where the media has access to almost everything within three seconds of its happening (if not before), cannot imagine the mentality of Church leadership being in the opposite direction. At times, they seem to say that nothing should be revealed except the Sunday Mass schedule.

Since I feel strongly that transparency is a great source of strength to most organizations, I feel even more strongly about its importance in regards to the Catholic Church—or any church, for that matter.

Where does the tendency to be secretive come from? In my opinion, it flows from a naïve and mistaken attitude of many church leaders that the faithful—the laity, the rank and file—simply cannot handle scandal, and that they must be protected from it. In our society, you begin to find out about reality and the difficulties in life by the time you reach puberty. By the time you are eighteen or twenty, you have seen virtually every negative issue that you're going to see between that age and the time that you die.

People learn very early that just as they are weak and frail and prone to mistakes, so also are their superiors. Even though leaders are burdened with awesome responsibilities, they are still prone to stumbling and falling. When I say falling, I don't just mean that the pastor may not have gotten the bulletin finished on time, but that he may not have finished it on time because he left with the organist!

Mistakes and failures on the part of leaders are always disappointing. Of course, when they are religious leaders, the pain and disappointment is more profound. Regardless, however, the laity has an innate ability to realize that they have centered their faith in Jesus of Nazareth, and not solely in some priest or religious woman or other authority figure.

When Pope John XXIII convened the first session of the Second Vatican council, it upset the cadre of church functionaries working in the Vatican with him (he always called them the "apostles of doom"), because they could see that bringing all those people together at one time was going to be a huge logistical problem, as well as the likelihood that this gathering would attract reporters like flies. The policy that was outlined at the beginning was that the bishops would meet from 9am-1pm for the main work session, and committees could meet in the afternoons. Over two thousand (~2300) bishops would attend. There were to be no press conferences, and the bishops were instructed to tell no one of what went on in the meetings. That was the frame of reference for Vatican bureaucrats in 1963. What does that say about how far from reality they were?

Of course, once the bishops actually met, that framework was rejected, and together they developed a better plan to communicate their ideas. *That mindset of secrecy is absurd!* Unfortunately, there is still a tremendous amount of that instinctive desire for secrecy in the upper echelon of the Church.

The tragic scandal of sexual abuse that occurred over the last two decades, and became visible only at the beginning of the year 2000, is largely due to secrecy. Priests would get into trouble (as most of them tend to be human beings, with the frailties and failures inherent therein), and when a scandal would occur, it would be taken care of under the table. Regretfully, we bishops were catastrophic failures in how we handled this tragic situation. In fairness, however, it needs to be known that the bishops at this time were receiving terribly ineffective professional advice from two sources: the doctors and the lawyers. The psychiatrists would frequently assure a bishop that after a brief rehab program, the priest could successfully return to active duty. Lawyers all across the country advised the bishops to hunker down- refuse to speak to the parents, and to leave everything in the hands of the attorneys. This put the Church in a siege position, bent on defending its own interest ahead of the interests of the victims. Added to all this is the fact that the Church is in the business of forgiveness and second chances. A bishop wouldn't bring charges against a priest. He couldn't fire them. The bishop would simply transfer the problem priest to a new location—a new parish—*and not tell the new parish and the new pastor that this guy has a problem.* The Church simply could not deal with this openly, and the effect of that was that it eventually grew into an explosion. Their secrecy not only did not succeed, but it literally blew up in their faces.

The fundamental principle here (and the civil society knows this so well) is that the cover-up is always viewed as a bigger problem than the original transgression. Transgressions out on the top of the table can be dealt with. Transgressions faced honestly and objectively can be handled. Problems that are covered up will reappear as an explosion, and be far more destructive. Ask Mr. Nixon about that.

I can only speak for myself, but I want to express my profound sadness, disappointment and shame for the fact that this great institution to which

I have given my life has failed so miserably on this issue. I feel confident, however, that although we were pathetically slow learners, we are putting it behind us, and I hope in the future the Roman Catholic Church will be a perfect example of sensitivity and concern for victims of all types.

AND WHAT'S THE PROBLEM?

"Can you hear me now?"

In many ways, the Roman Catholic Church is the most amazing organization on the planet. It has united one billion, two hundred million people, voluntarily drawn from hundreds of nations. The Church utilizes hundreds of languages, thousands of dialects and countless cultures, and has kept them united together in the central message of Jesus Christ. Despite these accomplishments, however, the Church does not score well in its method of communicating with the modern world. Universal communication actually should not be a problem, because the whole thrust of the Church in our theology is as a community of faith reaching out to the whole world, for all time, to give people the message that Jesus of Nazareth brought about God's love for the human family. So, really, the Church is overwhelmingly about communication.

When it runs hospitals, when it runs clinics, when it takes little kids into orphanages, the Church is really just communicating the love of God made concrete by a particular community, in a particular place. But, in my opinion, the Church today is doing a very poor job of communicating. It has been for a long time. And that's due to the fact that the people who are in leadership positions in the Church are, in my opinion, at times more concerned with authority and jurisdiction than they are with communicating the message of Jesus. They would deny that absolutely. They would say, "No, that's absolutely wrong. We are protecting the faithful from scandals that could undermine their faith."

The governmental structure, I think, has worked very well. But I believe with all my heart that the way certain things are being done is undercutting the Church's mission to convey the message of Jesus Christ. The leadership must join the modern world, continuing efforts to recognize that transparency is absolutely required in this day and time. The pope and the bishops should change their views regarding secrecy, and recognize the fact that the laity has understood how to handle scandals since the time of St. Peter.

When people say "Roman Catholic," what do they see? If they are outside the Church, they may respect the Church for its size, or for its age; they may respect it for all the good things it does, but they don't see the Roman Catholic Church as a loving, caring, nurturing entity from the outside. Many people do see it in this positive light from the inside, and happily, it is that way. But others also see the Church as a fortress that is more concerned about maintaining the system regardless of how people may get hurt. My hope for this developing Church is that it will more effectively communicate its love and concern for human pain and suffering, and attempt to draw people together from all across the world to build a faith community founded on truth and love.

CHARITY

"Today I call your attention to the special needs of those who are emotionally disturbed, mentally ill, or developmentally disabled. Yes, these, too, are our brothers and sisters. They need understanding and love. We, as the followers of Jesus, should be the first to offer those gifts to them."
—Bishop John McCarthy's Pastoral Letter on Mental Health

As I have said repeatedly, the Roman Catholic Church is an enormous worldwide institution, with over a billion voluntary members. While not all are actively practicing Catholics, if they were checking into a hospital and were asked about their faith, they would check the box for Roman Catholics. What I am about to say about the Catholic Church applies almost equally to other faith communities, whether they be Protestants, Jews, or Muslims, but I am specifically referring to our Roman Catholic worldwide community. Our Church spread around the world does an enormous number of different things, but most of them can be broken down into three groups: worship, education, and "lessening suffering."

Worship, from a theological perspective, is the most important thing that the Church does. We are created by God and redeemed by Jesus Christ. And that should call out of us a loving response to honor and show appreciation for what God is and what God has done for us. So worship is tremendously important theologically.

You cannot, however, bring other people to worship with you unless you teach your faith. And so the second main activity inside the church all across the world is education. Education ranges from great schools like the University of Notre Dame or the University of Paris on down through smaller colleges and high schools and elementary schools. And it includes other forms of education like discussion clubs, book clubs, and even magazines whose prime purpose is to teach church beliefs and practices. The fundamental level of religious education is the family. The Church needs to complete the basic parochial structure by adding social ministry. And when that breaks down, everything else breaks down.

The third component of the Church could be called by many different names, but the way I define it is the "lessening of pain." When I'm talking to people about this subject, I always like to talk about St. Theresa's Parish in Houston. St. Theresa's made a great impact on me. It was the first affluent parish in which I ever served for an extended period of time. Working in an affluent parish teaches that money isn't everything. Affluent families don't have the suffering that comes from hunger, and don't usually have the suffering that comes from financial insecurity. However, there still may be a failure to love or other misfortune, in the form of bitterness, alcoholism, drug addiction, divorce, domestic violence, and/or incest. These troubles are found frequently in very affluent areas. So when you talk about charity, people usually think about food baskets and getting the light bill paid. Yes, those things need to be done. They are tremendously important acts of charity. But if you use a larger umbrella called the "lessening of pain," then helping people overcome other difficulties is a major component to the life of the Church. It doesn't take place usually until teaching and worship are already set up. When a parish is set up with a Mass schedule, a baptismal schedule, and a catechetical program, but without a method to get the lights turned on or a program for drug abuse assistance, the parish will fail in important aspects of its ministry.

That is the theological explanation of why the Church—wherever it is really strong and flourishing—allocates a lot of its resources to lessening pain, helping people improve their situation, and, as is often the case, protecting people. The way the Catholic Church fought for labor unions' rights back in the 1930s and 1940s was a glorious chapter in American Catholic history. When the Church ultimately got on the right side of the race issue, it was another bright chapter, but one that we came to slowly. This of course is the ideal, what we shoot for. But there have been many times in our history that we have fallen way below that ideal.

For example, one of the saddest books that I have ever read was *King Leopold's Ghost*, which told the story of the horrible cruel colonial policies in the Belgium Congo. The Belgium King found a little strip of land along the Atlantic ocean, stepped onto the land with soldiers, and conquered about a third of Africa, claiming that third of Africa for Belgium. And it became the Belgium Congo. What this Catholic/Christian country did was to go in and slaughter elephants like mad and cut off their tusks because the ivory was so valuable.

And then, with the modernization of cars, the need for rubber exploded. So they would go in with soldiers to a village or two, and bring all the people together. They would build a stockade, and put the women and children in the stockade. Then they would give all the men buckets, and show them how to cut trees and draw rubber. They executed thousands, and caused diseases that killed thousands. It's a terrible story. And finally, at around the turn of the century, the world leaned on Belgium to stop this cruelty.

When we fall way below the ideal, we are acting in variance with our principles. You will never find the Christian tradition espousing cruelty. You might find individual Christians who are being cruel, but it is never the position of the Church.

What should the everyday layperson be focusing on for their charity? Well, the three arms of the church are worship, education, and the lessening of pain. In our own individual lives, we need to do those same three things. We worship when we say morning prayers, we worship when we say the Rosary. We worship when we go to Mass. We worship when we sit in an easy chair in our room and look at the wall thinking about reality and wondering, "Is there really a God out there? Yes, I think so. I'm going to act like there is. That's the safe way." Those are all acts of worship.

When you spend time talking to your children about Jesus, when you perform acts of kindness, these are forms of teaching about how we ought to live. Teaching and lessening pain can overlap. If you envision one of your roles in your life as being a follower of Jesus, you will perform acts to lessen pain that you become aware of around you. That has tremendous educational impact. Such acts must be carried out with great sensitivity free of any sustentation. It's like your morning offering: you do it all to worship God.

How do we find a balance between what we're doing with our treasure as well as our time and talents? How much money should we give our parish, our local food pantry, or an emergency relief effort after a disaster? How much time and talent should we be designating to needs outside our immediate family each week? There is no formula. You must find your own comfort level. *But you can't have a comfort level unless you think about it.* You might ask yourself questions. You might say, "We gave x dollars away last year, and I did this much pro bono work, and I have to balance that with my long-term plans for my children's education and maintaining my elderly father." If you look at your resources and all of your obligations, there is almost always some "fat" in there. I think a good rule of thumb might be something like this: You give primarily from the fat, but ideally, you'll offer enough to feel a small pinch. But you don't need give away your house. And you shouldn't feel guilty about having a nice house…but it wouldn't hurt to offer the use of it for your favorite charity's fundraiser.

HOW DO PRIESTS LIVE?

"The priesthood had tremendous attraction for me.
I saw it as a happy life."

—*Bishop John McCarthy*

Let's talk about the priesthood as lived today in the United States. There are fewer than 40,000 Catholic priests, and the median age is something like fifty. How are they doing? How are their lives lived?

Priests are divided into basically two groups: priests who belong to religious orders, and priests who are ordained for service in a particular diocese. The popular names for these groups are "order priests" and "diocesan priests." They actually overlap to a great extent.

When people think of order priests, they probably think of missionaries and teachers; most communities specialize in one or the other of those fields. The Jesuits, Franciscans and Dominicans are examples of religious orders. Diocesan priests are typically thought of in the context of Parish service. In point of fact, we have Diocesan priests teaching in universities, and order priests running parishes, and both Diocesan and Order priests going to foreign nations, so there is clearly overlap between the two.

In any given situation, you might be hard put to tell the difference between them. One difference is that the order priests take special vows. We call them "Religious" because the word religious comes from the Latin word, "relegare," which means, "to bind." When priests go into a Religious community or order, they invariably take the three vows of poverty, chastity, and obedience. Occasionally, a community like the Jesuits will have a fourth vow of special obedience to the Bishop of Rome. The order priest takes a vow of poverty, but all of his basic needs are taken care of. The Diocesan priest gets paid—not a real salary, but more of a stipend. The order priest takes a vow of special obedience to his bishop, and to any bishop in whose diocese that he is working. The order priest is also committed to chastity—the order is by a solemn, public vow—and the diocesan priest makes an implicit promise that occurs on the day of his ordination. Essentially, this vow is the same, however.

The vast majority of all priests in the United States, whether they are order priests or diocesan priests, serve parishes. That's where the Church is. The parish is where the Church is Incarnate, made flesh, made concrete in a particular part of the vineyard. East St. Louis, East L.A., West Houston— that's where the people live, and that's where they gather to worship. That's where problems manifest themselves. That's where their education takes place, along with all that goes on in the religious community that we call a parish.

The organizational core of that parish is nearly invariably the priest. Without him, you don't have the authority of the Church passing through the Bishop to the lives of the people. Without the parish priest, you don't have a sacramental life. You'll have a gathering of Catholics, but you won't have a living church.

Parish priests are faced with many problems today. There are twenty million more Catholics, and twenty thousand fewer priests than there were fifty years ago. The workload of a priest is awesome. But you know what happens when your workload is absolutely impossible and unbearable, and you simply can't do it any longer? Some people just give up and quit working. They are overwhelmed, and simply feel no expenditure of energy is going to make any difference. There are a certain number of priests that, faced with this seemingly insurmountable workload, just cut back themselves. Sadly, they become what I refer to as "top of the bulletin" priests. They are present for weekend confessions, masses, weddings, and baptisms, but lack initiative and enthusiasm for expending their energy to build up the body of Christ, our Church.

The others (happily the vast majority) keep working diligently, and often they're exhausted. They don't see any relief coming. They're older, the work is growing, and their numbers are falling. That's a bad combination.

There are two wonderful byproducts of this: One is that many of these extraordinary men struggle along in true heroism. The other gift is that the laity, most of who have been ignored by the Church for centuries in terms of any type of leadership in the Church, have come forward by the tens of thousands.

Lay people have become first-rate theologians, teachers, business managers, and you name it! The laity is doing an excellent job of fulfilling all those jobs that don't require Holy Orders. Ultimately, although we're short-handed by traditional standards, the fact is that we're functioning, and functioning very well, all things considered.

One thing that an individual parishioner can do for the parish priest is to understand that he has a monumental problem that never goes away— *he never gets off duty*. Please, never say to a priest on Sunday, "Oh, Father, you must be really tired since this is the one day you work." This sounds like a tiny psychological issue, but it's a big irritation for priests. In my experience, no priest works forty hours per week. They either work a mere ten to twelve hours (those few "top of the bulletin" priests), or more commonly, they work an overloaded eighty to ninety hours. People see the priest living in the rectory next to the parish, and they picture that as the priest never having to go to work. He lives there, and the Catholic world comes to him. From the point of view of the priest, it is the opposite- he never gets time off. If it's your day off or your vacation, and a parishioner dies, or is injured, you don't take that day off. When a boy is shot, or someone gets a tough sentence in court, or someone loses a child, you cannot wall yourself off. If you're a REAL priest, you toss aside your own plans, and go take care of the people in need.

I think maybe the most important thing lay people can do is to accept the humanity of their priests. Recognize that priests still get frightened when they face surgery. Remember that they get as tired as everyone else. They have good and bad days, just like everyone else. When a priest is noble and good, all's right with the world because, well, he's supposed to be—it's expected. When he does something second-rate or immoral—it's "how could he have done that?"

I don't mean that we should tolerate sinfulness, but let's not be shocked and surprised that a certain percentage of priests a certain percentage of the time will do something less than noble. The strain on a conscientious priest frequently makes him more easily irritated, and undermines his self-discipline. Priests can be sometimes blinded to the terrible damage incurred by any improper actions on his part—a show of temper, an immoral suggestion, or an off-color comment or joke. Seven years in a seminary does not a saint make!

So, please, be patient with your priests. If they're good priests- and the vast majority are- be aware that they are under constant strain. Take the time to ask them how they are doing—don't just wait until you need something from them to connect. And don't forget to pray for them.

THESE ARE A FEW OF MY FAVORITE THINGS NUNS!

"Not all of us can do great things.
But we can do small things with great love."
—*Mother Teresa*

As the Roman Catholic Church attempts to fulfill its mission by bringing the message and love of Jesus Christ into the world, I often stop and ponder its many advantages and resources. For example, I think the Church's governmental structure of dividing the whole world into dioceses and parishes is excellent. Even if you live in Timbuktu, you have a pastor. He may be far away, and you may not really know him, but on our books, someone is responsible for you. I believe the liturgy of the Church is another extraordinary strength. The list could go on and on, but I want to share what for me has been an extraordinary gift to the Church in the 19th and 20th centuries. What is this precious gift? Nuns!

Tens of thousands of Catholic women have so generously offered themselves to the work of Jesus Christ as vowed religious women. Maybe I should have made this whole book about them! At the very least, however, I can tell you about a few extraordinary sisters that made an awesome impression on me. Know that these sisters are the tip of the iceberg—a few individual cases of the women who are truly countless in number.

Let me tell you first about **Sister Kathy Foster**, who I met while I was serving as the auxiliary bishop in Galveston/Houston. Sister Kathy came to me terribly distraught because she was seeing situations in which totally dependent infants were being suddenly abandoned. The mother of tiny 14-month-old Billy is in jail, and the INS has deported the father. A courageous neighbor has had the child for two days, but is getting desperate. Sister Kathy Foster tells me that if she could only get a four-bedroom house, she could begin to take care of such children. I gave her a mere $3,000 and the use of such a house. Fast-forward a few decades…I saw her financial report last year. She has fourteen NEW houses and a budget of $6 million taking care of about 125 kids. Amen, amen!

Sister Maureen O'Connell is dear to my heart. She is kind and gentle, but exudes real strength. In fact, before becoming a nun, Sr. Maureen was a cop in Chicago for thirteen years! In that role, she saw the terrible suffering of women being released from the prison system with no help and no support, which understandably generated frequent returns to prison. Sister Maureen, now a Dominican sister, opened Angela House in 2001—a home for women in this challenging transition after incarceration. I am continually amazed at how she continues to do such extraordinary work with pathetically limited resources. Feel free to send her a donation!

Did you ever know **Sister Mary Louis**? If you did not, consider that a great loss! She taught me in the 7th grade at All Saints School, over in Houston Heights. The school served a poor area. There was no library, no science area, not even a cafeteria. Sr. Mary Louis was teaching approximately forty-two students, and had direct personal involvement with every one of us, continuing for years after we had moved on to higher grades. The girls thought she was the wisest person they had ever known. Truth be told, all of us boys were in love with her, because she was so beautiful. All those students were so impressed with her, in fact, that we continued to meet years and years later, as long as she was alive (she passed away in 2001).

Back in about 1964, my good friend Archbishop Joseph Fiorenza and I rode horses up into the Guatemalan Cuchumatanes Mountains. We had heard that something wonderful was up there, and we wanted to see for ourselves. High up in the mountains (after a six-hour horseback ride) we met **Sister Rose Cordis**, Maryknoll Missioner. There we saw a complete hospital with operating facilities, x-ray machines, and virtually everything that was available at that time, along with two wards—one for men and one for women. This hospital was the only hospital for hundreds of miles. How did she do it? *How did she even get the equipment up there?* I don't know! But I've always found that dedicated nuns have the capacity to do the impossible.

Last but certainly not least, let me share the story of a local Austin favorite. When I came to Austin thirty years ago, I quickly became involved with the wonderful Seton health care system, truly a gem in Texas. In the process, I met a rather elderly nun, **Sr. Philomena Feltz**. Mind you, I knew she was elderly not because of the way she moved (she was FAST!), but because she had already been at Seton Hospital for over five or six decades. Sr. Philomena walked the corridors of Seton for decades, bringing on, with the best of the medical community, physical health and bodily survival. But, along with those packages, she also brought faith, joy, laughter, and hope. She exuded those qualities, and people who had the privilege of being close to her sensed them and were strongly influenced by her in their own life.

What I remember best is that she had the wonderful reputation of "borrowing" food from the hospital kitchen in the rock bottom of the Depression, and distributing it from the back door to hungry people! Sister Philomena Feltz, DC, is a member of the 400-year-old Daughters of Charity community. Until they were modernized after the council, their great symbol was their wonderful bonnets that looked like twin sailboats above their heads! I think about them when I drive past the Dell Children's Hospital, because the architect topped off the tower with these bonnets of the Daughters of Charity.

We give thanks to God for these amazing women and ask our Lord to continue blessing their work, as well as the wonderful work of all our Catholic Sisters!

HOW ARE BISHOPS CHOSEN?

"When I worked for the Texas Catholic Conference, I worked for eleven bishops. Ten of them liked me."
—*Bishop John McCarthy*

Everyone knows there are bishops, but how are bishops made bishops?

The Church has set up a method for choosing bishops. First, though, let's look at how leaders are chosen in the secular world.

There are various means of choosing leaders, beginning with fighting. This person knocks that person out, so he is the strongest, and therefore, the leader. In our country, we have elections. Bribery can place a person in office in some settings. Any of these means can produce conflict and bitterness. Look at Hilary and Obama—they're from the same party, but they certainly don't vacation together.

The Church has developed a system that attempts to avoid the pitfalls of other systems while it seeks to identify possible candidates for the office. It works like this. Every year, shortly after the great feast of Easter, the Bishops of a province gather, and share their thoughts about various priests' good work in their diocese. They discuss whether these men should be considered for the office of Bishop. They discuss those names, vote secretly, and then forward those names to the papal ambassador (nuncio) in Washington, D.C. The papal nuncio gathers these names together, and starts a file for each province. Nothing may happen for years after that.

Suddenly there's a death, or a Bishop is moved out of state, and an opening is created. The papal nuncio then contacts the Bishops of the province where there is a vacancy, even though they've already sent in their reports. He asks who they think would do the best job, given the specific diocese with its specific issues at that time. The Bishops of the province send him the names they would suggest—again, secretly. You can't tell anyone you even sent in the names.

At this point, the nuncio gathers all these, reviews them, and then makes his own list. The nuncio will know priests in the province, and his list may or may not overlap or agree with the two lists that the Bishops of the province have already sent. At any rate, the list from the nuncio is sent to Rome to the Congregation for Bishops. The Congregation then makes its own list. To clarify, the province Bishops make their initial suggestions—say A, B, and C—then they make their suggestions at the time of the opening—say B, C, and D. The papal nuncio then adds his suggestions—D, E, and F—and the Congregation sends their list—perhaps D, G, and H. All these choices and lists are sent to the Pope. The Pope doesn't have to pay attention to any of the recommendations.

Now, in point of fact, the Pope would probably rubber-stamp the recommendations of the whole process, nine times out of ten, and especially if it is a consistent recommendation from all three sources. There are about thirty-five hundred dioceses in the world, and there's no way for the Pope to know all of them intimately. But when it comes to New York, Rio de Janeiro, Tokyo, Berlin, or London, or any other big worldwide center, then the Pope is directly involved. The Pope might easily pass over all the recommendations and place a different person who he thinks is the best man for the job.

So, that's it in a nutshell. We try to have a fair system, but we are all humans. As such, who likes whom and who dislikes whom are factors in the selection process.

So many times, when bishops meet strangers not familiar with the inner workings of the Catholic Church, they are asked not only how are bishops elected, but what do bishops do? Traditional Catholics will tell you that a bishop comes around periodically, wearing a funny hat and celebrating a sacrament called Confirmation. Others will quickly point out that their bishop writes frequently, and it's usually letters asking for money. Actually, both of these things are true. The Bishop is responsible for many diocesan activities, and the resources to accomplish those activities have to be drawn from the body of the faithful. So, it's often the Bishop's job to inform people of this need or that obligation or responsibility, and ask if they would please step forward and be generous. The funny hat and Confirmation are less accurate. The Bishop is the "ordinary minister" of the sacrament of confirmation. "Ordinary" is a word for law or power. If the Bishop wants to delegate a priest to confirm for him, he can do that. This is simply one of the regular visible activities of a bishop.

The Bishop of a mid-sized diocese is responsible for one to two hundred parishes, half that many elementary schools, a half dozen or more high schools, a number of hospitals and clinics, and maybe a university or two. In addition, he must provide leadership to all the priests and deacons in the diocese, support and affirmation to all the religious women in the diocese, and maintain the face of the Church in dealing with the larger community—the diocesan city or smaller towns.

To do all this and to try to keep most people happy at the same time is quite a challenge. When you see a Bishop leave office at the end of his career, you're going to see a man who is ready to transfer the burden to another, but hopefully satisfied that he has done a great deal of good in a difficult position. At least, that's how I felt upon passing my torch.

WHAT DO CARDINALS
ACTUALLY DO?

"When Cardinal Spellman died, the search for his replacement was what I call 'the Great American Catholic Talent Search.' It was such an important position. They officially looked for the new Cardinal all over the world, and yet they found him two doors down the hall on the same floor. Cardinal Terry Cook—who literally lived next door—replaced him."
—*Bishop John McCarthy*

Who are the Cardinals? It's not a baseball team, although they do wear red. The Roman Catholic Cardinals are an interesting group of older men who either have jobs in the Vatican, or are scattered in major cities across the world. Cardinals are Catholic men who decided to become priests, were later promoted to the office of bishop or archbishop, and then received the honor of being appointed as Cardinals in the Roman Catholic Church.

To be a cardinal is really not a difficult job. Your main responsibility is to elect a new Pope when one succumbs, which means, on average, going off to Rome every ten or fifteen years. However, since the Church is so tremendously important in the lives of one billion, two hundred million Roman Catholics, selecting the head of the Church is very, very important. Although I said their job description as a cardinal is fairly easy, almost all of them actually have two different sets of responsibilities. A man may be a cardinal in the Vatican and eligible to vote for the next Pope, but he may also be the Archbishop of Sao Paolo in Brazil or the Archbishop of New York City, or the Archbishop of Tokyo. The men who are placed in these extremely important dioceses across the world are first given those jobs, and then later find themselves appointed Cardinal. These different and overlapping titles do not arrive at the same time.

I occasionally find myself interacting with a group of people that I don't know very well, and who may or may not be Catholic, but especially now with the resignation of Pope Benedict, I am frequently asked, "How are cardinals chosen?" Because they get a lot of press, most people know that they exist, but simply don't know much about them.

Well, you can't tell the story of cardinals without going back a thousand years. That's true of everything else about the Church, isn't it? So, when did the office originate? In the third and fourth century, in the city of Rome. As the Popes began to die—and most of the Popes were martyred in the first two hundred and fifty years of the Church's existence—the priests of the Christian communities of Rome would come together and decide who should be the new Bishop of Rome. They would not necessarily have used that terminology, but they were voting for whoever would be the new leader of the Church in Rome. This went on for most of a thousand years, until most of northern Europe began to realize the importance and power vested in the papacy. Then the Archbishop of London, the Archbishop of Paris, and the Archbishop of Stuttgart decided that they should have a say about who became Pope, since the papacy had so much jurisdiction over them. And so they began to appoint men in these prestigious cities of Northern Europe as cardinals. When European civilization jumped across the Atlantic and began to develop in North and South America, this policy was continued, although until the recent past, the vast majority of Cardinals have been in Europe.

The funny thing is that when a Pope expires, the Cardinals begin to move to Rome as fast as they can. You can watch your television set and see them process into the Sistine Chapel to cast the first vote on the new Pope. That's not the just the Archbishop of Paris or Tokyo or Rio de Janeiro, but that's the pastor of Santa Sabina, or the pastor of Santa Maria. In modern times, as the Church appoints the position of cardinal, each cardinal is also made the pastor of a current parish in the city of Rome. So, the reality that took place in the fourth century of the pastors of Rome convening to elect the Bishop of Rome is still going on in the third millennium, because they are the true pastors of Rome. Each one has his own church, of which he is the pastor. Now, they don't typically perform weddings or handle day-to-day activities of the parish, but they are expected to do certain things for their parish. It's a beautifully symbolic concept, and reflects the Church's tremendous commitment to tradition.

Cardinal—the word itself—means, "hinge." This refers to the swinging from the old to the new Pope. From the late middle ages until the middle of the twentieth century, the number of cardinals was limited to seventy, and the vast majority were Europeans. Most, in fact, were Italians. Why so many Italians? The cardinals were the top administrators of the universal Church, (all the different offices and bureaucracies of the Vatican were headed by cardinals) and they physically needed to be in Rome. These top administrators couldn't do their jobs effectively from across the world in Mexico City or Berlin. Therefore, we have always maintained a sizable cadre of cardinals residing in Rome.

Of course, another contributing factor is that the language of the Vatican is Italian. Therefore, since the Italians were physically there, and they were comfortable with the language, they frequently got themselves appointed cardinals. That's true of the Vatican bureaucracy. When you're talking about cardinals scattered across the world in the major cities, they do not have full-time responsibilities back in Rome. They're on committees that might require them to go to Rome two or three times per year, but other than that, they're expected to be running their respective dioceses outside of Rome.

At the present time, there are around one hundred and twenty cardinals eligible to vote for a new Pope (because cardinals must be younger than 80 years old to vote.) One hundred and fifteen cardinals were eligible in 2013 to vote when Pope Benedict XVI surprisingly announced his plan to retire. The modern Popes have tried to scatter the cardinals -with some degree of fairness- around the world. The United States has the second largest number after Italy. (Italy has around twenty-five, and we have eight or nine.)

The Pope has referred to the College of Cardinals as his Senate. Honestly, I'm not sure that's a good description, because they are all there because either the Pope or his predecessor appointed them individually. If a person is the source of your position and your power and responsibility, you might not be inclined to be extraordinarily frank or honest with him.

Every country in the world with a good number of dioceses has the Bishops organized into a national conference, and to me, our Holy Father would get much better service for advice and administrative assistance if his one hundred and fifty bishops were elected by their peers in the different countries in which they live. I've made this suggestion for years, but I don't see any stampede in that general direction.

LET'S ALL JUST GET ALONG

"There was a delightful explosion of ecumenical activity across the world immediately following the Second Vatican Council. New relationships developed between virtually every major Protestant denomination and the Catholic Church. It was a wonderful period of growth for ecumenism. The times have changed and the quest for unity has slowed, and the Roman Catholic Church has circled the wagons again. A sad situation."

—Bishop John McCarthy

Ecumenism is a word drawn from the root of the Greek word for "universal." *Ecumenism describes the ideal or hope that the Christian churches could be open to each other, and improve communication and cooperation with the hope of ultimately being united according to the will of Jesus.* In his last discourse to the apostles, He willed that all of his followers would be one, the way He was one with His Father and the Holy Spirit. Ecumenism does not refer to improving relations between Christians and Muslims, Jews, or any other faiths outside of the Christian family (although, of course, that is another important goal.) Today, ecumenism specifically refers to a movement of greater unity among the Christian churches. Cooperative work between the other groups and Christians is certainly of great importance as well, but is referred to as inter-religious dialogue.

In 1965, ecumenism became a really hot topic in the worldwide community. Roman Catholics who had been aloof for centuries in terms of interfaith cooperation and understanding suddenly rejoined the conversation at the table. The Catholic Church did it in a way that it so frequently does—after centuries of withdrawal, the Church moved very quickly and made ecumenism a major thrust of its relationship with the larger world following Vatican II. Virtually every diocese in the world set up ecumenical commissions at the diocesan level, and many parishes chose to enter into a wide range of cooperative projects with their Protestant neighbors.

This experience was invigorating for both sides, and soon a tremendous degree of optimism began to permeate ecumenical dialogue. Common structures such as the Texas Conference of Churches were established in order to foster openness, dialogue, and cooperation.

The same excitement was going on at the international level, where the Vatican established commissions or other entities to deal in a very concrete way with specific religious groups. For example, there were the Roman Catholic/Anglican and Roman Catholic/Lutheran dialogues, but others were established as well. These international groups brought together the best theologians from all over the world, and wonderful progress was made in providing a deeper understanding of the splits that had produced the Protestant Reformation in the 16th century. One of the happy byproducts left over from the early days of ecumenism is a deeper understanding that God's infinite love for every human being will carry us past our denominational handicaps, fences, and walls, and lift us up through the saving power of Jesus Christ to eternal life with God.

However, this wonderful progress did not go on forever. The Papacy was less than enthusiastic about some of the final documents developed by these commissions. It's hard for Catholic theologians to move forward enthusiastically when the brake is being slammed on from the Tiber. On the Protestant side, other events also contributed to the slowing of the process; for example, the Anglican decision to begin ordaining women to the priesthood. In fact, now they are preparing to move toward the ordination of women to the episcopacy (bishop level). Here in the United States, the Episcopalian decision to include homosexual priests further complicated things.

Given the slowdown at the international level and the national level, it was only a matter of time before the level of enthusiasm for ecumenical activities began to slow down at the local judicatories.

Today things are very quiet in the world of ecumenism.

We still have those words from our blessed Lord challenging his follow-ers to be united. What should a person who is really committed to bring-ing that divine desire to fruition do? I am of the opinion that when a large number of lay people rekindle their interest in Christian unity, the bureau-cratic ecclesiastical structures will respond! Speaking as a Roman Catholic, I must recognize that Jesus of Nazareth died for my Protestant friends as well as for Catholics. He wants all of us—Baptists, Lutherans, Episcopalians, Presbyterians, and Catholics—to unite again as His people. We need to recognize that the effect of combining all the Christian faiths has truly awe-some potential for goodness. This resource for a better world should not be neglected. This potential grace should be utilized to the utmost! Jesus chal-lenges us to be united, but this unity takes an increase in virtue and work.

A Catholic cannot improve his relationships and understanding of other Christian faiths unless he has a deep understanding of his own. This under-standing is essential in order to grasp the points of agreement and disagree-ment with another church, and my friends, this requires work. Ecumenism calls for an increased study and understanding of Catholicism, and it calls for openness, understanding, and empathy for the other churches. Needless to say what's true on the Catholic side is true on the Protestant side as well.

First of all, many of the differences between us are in the area of struc-ture, discipline, and culture. When we can isolate these superficial differ-ences, we are able to come to grips with the major theological points that are continuing to cause our separation—and actually, these are few in number!

The great truths of Christianity are:

- The existence of an infinite triune God, Who is the creator and sustainer of all that exists.
- That among the creatures that God brought into existence was one that we called man or human, and he was created for the purpose of sharing God's life.
- That intended purpose was frustrated by the introduction of sin—a rupture between the Creator and the creature, thereby separating man from the purpose of his existence.
- This separation is overcome by our infinitely loving God, Who, in the person of Jesus, comes among us, teaching us how to live and offering Himself as an infinite atonement for the sins of the human family.

These four basic truths are shared by virtually all Christian faiths. It is within the fifth truth that differences are generated. That fifth principle is that Jesus Christ commissioned the apostles to go forth and to carry the above-mentioned principles to the ends of the earth, and that He would stay with those who did this work until the end of time. That community that has the responsibility to carry forth that message is what nearly all of us call the Church, but that's where the serious and historically bitter conflict has developed. The work of ecumenism should be to stress the overwhelming unity that we already have on those first four principles, and to continue open dialogue until we can come closer to each other on number five, the Church, and develop one Church that all can believe in, that all will support, and that will provide community and support for all.

God wills it!

OUR RELATIONSHIP
WITH JEWISH PEOPLE

"The inscription of the charge against him read,
THE KING OF THE JEWS."

—*Mark 15:26*

When Christian people stop and think about the Jews, many different thoughts come to mind. I hope and believe that the vast majority are positive, but regretfully, one thought in particular can be very negative. Among the positive ideas relating to the Jews are stability, historicity, faithfulness, and endurance in the face of adversity. If anyone knows the experience of the Jews, they know the accuracy of those words.

The negative concept that some Christians regretfully associate with the Jewish people is the death of Jesus of Nazareth. That concept has dominated Christian-Jewish relations from the first century all the way along the timeline until the middle of the 20th century. It is true that Jesus was tried in a Jewish court. However, it was the Roman governor and the Roman soldiers that put Jesus to death—but more about that later.

The Christian reaction to the death of Jesus has been tragically out of proportion to the simple historic facts of what occurred in Jerusalem in the spring of what we tend to call the year 33 AD. That event so stained the Jewish reputation as to unleash 1800 years of persecution and oppression that stretches beyond the imagination. This is tragedy upon tragedy, century after century.

I am thrilled by the fact that Pope Paul VI, John Paul II, Benedict XVI, and now, hopefully, Pope Francis, have worked and are continuing efforts

to apologize for and to lessen the tension that regretfully still resides within portions of the Christian camp.

How should a Roman Catholic properly respond to the Jewish reality in our cities and neighborhoods? First of all, our response should be respectful. We're dealing with American citizens who have the same rights as everyone else, and pay taxes, and frankly, cost the social services of this country nearly nothing. That is a real contribution. Secondly, we should have appreciation for the fact that despite all they have endured, Jews do not retaliate with hatred or any obvious desire for revenge. Thirdly, we have to respect the essence of the Jewish faith, because everything that they believe, we believe. They believe in one God, the Author of all creation. They believe in the Ten Commandments. They believe in strong family life, and as a people, they are extraordinarily concerned about contributing to a more just society.

I have had the privilege and delight of working with Jewish people at the local, state, and national level, as well as with many Jewish individuals throughout the last half-century. I found I could always turn to them with confidence, and that their sensitivity to injustice would give my projects a positive and generous response. My experience has given me, John McCarthy, the qualities of response that I referred to above—respecting their virtues, thanking God for their generosity, being open to sharing life with them in this great country, and bonding with the Jews as a people who share my basic beliefs about almighty God.

Do we need to convert them? In my opinion, absolutely NOT! The Jews were truly chosen by almighty God to be a special instrument in His plan to bring salvation to the whole human family. That plan was fulfilled by the children of Jacob, the tribe of Judah, the family of King David, the town of Bethlehem, and Mary and Joseph. We see God's plan moving forward as a divine trajectory toward the birth of Jesus. While as Christians we can regret the failure of Jews to accept Him at the time of His arrival, we cannot deny the extraordinary importance that they played in the unraveling of the story. Although they do not accept Jesus, their faith in God is extraordinary in the face of the abuse that they have taken at the hands of misdirected Christians.

We believe that salvation is through Jesus Christ, but that means also that we believe that the salvific acts of Jesus (principally his death, resurrection and ascension) are of such infinite value that by themselves they atone adequately for all human sinfulness. So, whether it be Jews, or Muslims, or other non-Christians, the potential for salvation is achieved by Jesus two thousand years ago. What is necessary for everyone is to want to do what he or she thinks God wants him or her to do in terms of living good lives. The Church calls this an "implicit baptism of desire," and it is a saving reality.

What about a marriage between a Catholic and a Jew? How should that work? Let me tell you point-blank, any time two people marry who have serious religious views which are not in unity with each other, one of the single strongest possible bonds of the marriage is simply not present. Does that mean such a marriage cannot succeed? Not at all, but it will require much greater patience, forbearance, and tact.

I find there is basic cultural unity between Catholics and Jews. Both of us have a sense of history. Both believe strongly in current divine action within the human story. We adopt one moral code, which was brought down from Mt. Sinai. I have found when there are inter-religious meetings that there is a natural affinity between the Catholic and Jewish delegates. I'm proud of that, and wish we would build on it!

Despite our commonality, Catholics are woefully ignorant of Jewish beliefs and Jewish structures. Tragically, they are especially uninformed about the terrible history of anti-Semitism, so much of which was generated by Catholics throughout history. I feel confident that in today's society, those outdated and misguided beliefs are definitely behind us. We are blessed to live in a time where, in the Western culture at least, there has been a wonderful openness to all types of minorities and groups that had been previously disallowed full participation in the main thrusts of society.

LEAVING THE STONES BEHIND

"Stone throwing is risky!"

Ordinarily, it would be hard to precisely pick my favorite part of the Bible, because I love all the scenes in it about the public life of Jesus and the parables that He taught. They are filled with dramatic scenes where He manifests one or another of His aspects, both human and divine. The New Testament is an endless source of imagery.

However, I have to admit that I do have one particular favorite scene in the life of our Lord that I love beyond most of the others. I'm referring to the vignette that is generally thought of as "the woman caught in adultery." Everyone knows the scene. It's very dramatic. As usual, Jesus is teaching a crowd, a large gathering of people who have come to hear for themselves the amazing words emanating from this carpenter from Nazareth.

Suddenly, there is a commotion, and at the outer edges of the crowd, people are being shoved back to make way for a number of men who are pushing and dragging a woman toward the center where Jesus stands. When they reach the open area in front of Jesus, this woman is hurled down to the ground. One or another of the men who has arrested her and dragged her forward says with the definitive voice of a Supreme Court judge, "This woman has been caught in adultery. According to our law, she must be stoned to death."

These men, already enemies of our Lord, think that they have Him in a bind. The crowds see him as kind and merciful, but the Law of Moses must be obeyed. If he does not condemn her to death, he's not following Mosaic Law. If he approves of the execution, he will be seen as cruel and heartless. At this point, I fall in love with the story. The text describes Jesus as He kneels down and begins to draw some type of design in the sand. Is He doodling? Writing messages or naming other sins? (This is, by the way, the only spot that I can think of in the Bible where Jesus is actually writing something.) Without looking up—still facing the ground—He says, "Let him who is without sin throw the first stone!" What a marvelous statement! What an all-encompassing freedom-giving explanation of the human condition.

There is evidently silence for a moment or two, and finally Jesus looks up. The men are gone, and the woman is alone. Jesus asks the woman, "Where are your accusers? Is there no one left to accuse you?" The woman replies, "There is no one." "Then neither will I. Go and sin no more," Jesus replies.

This story is profound, amazingly simple, and grabs at some of the deepest reactions and tendencies in the human condition. What we have here in a few short sentences is rash judgment, legalism, manipulation, cruelty, and the sin of male domination. Yet, in one simple sentence, it is all swept aside. The essence of Jesus comes right off the page of our Bible, and comes alive in our hearts and minds at this moment. "Let him who is without sin cast the first stone."

You know the other side of that? There is to be NO stone throwing. We know the tragic reality of human weakness, especially the way we rashly judge others so often, but this story makes us sit up straight and look not at those around us, but simply at ourselves.

Each of those weaknesses deserves a great deal of thought and discussion, but in this section I'll refer only to one: an unhappy combination of prejudice and judgmentalism. The men dragging the woman forward cry out in phony shock and scandal that "she has been caught in adultery". Adultery requires two people, yet there is no mention of the man, no condemnation of his actions, but only a desire to have this woman executed. Regretfully, that type of discrimination still goes on today- especially in other parts of this planet.

Do the words of Jesus forbid us from casting stones? Do not the actions of Jesus provide us with a wonderful motivation to be patient with the failures of the people around us? In the words of Mother Teresa, "If you judge people, you have no time to love them." I really believe that the basic message of this story could be lived by the great majority of us. The quality of life in our families, parishes, and greater society would be enhanced tremendously if we at least tried.

LOVE AND ACCEPTANCE FOR ALL

"Do you think that John the Baptist could easily fit into your neighborhood? Imagine that beard, the animal skins, and all those locusts! But God was working through him in an extraordinary way. Could that be happening in your neighborhood?"
— *Pastoral Letter on Mental Health*

In deepening our awareness of God's love for us, we develop within ourselves a capacity to love others to a greater extent. It is this human love responding to our awareness of divine love that brings joy and happiness into our lives. This lessening or the absence of love produces lives that are arid, selfish, and unhappy.

Let us seriously consider expanding our horizons where human love is concerned. Let us reach beyond a love that is limited to those closest to us. *Let us include those persons who have a desperate need for love but who frequently do not find it*, even among those of us who claim to be followers of Jesus of Nazareth.

Regretfully, our society seems to have an inordinate, perhaps immature, attachment to youthfulness, beauty, and health. These are excellent qualities, but most of us lack one or the other. Ultimately, all of us will lose all three. The worth of every human being is to be measured not by appearances or mental acumen, but rather by the fact that each of us is an extraordinarily unique being created by God and redeemed by Jesus Christ. Each person is of infinite worth because each of us was created in the image of God, "a little less than the angels."

While a large segment of our society may look with disdain and fear on persons who are different, the followers of Jesus should do the opposite.

Among our population, there are more than 35 million people who suffer from some type of mental or emotional disability. One family in four has been affected with this burden, and there is no parish in this diocese, or anywhere else, that does not have parishioners who carry the burden of mental disabilities or emotional illness. Needing understanding, support, and love, they all too frequently experience rejection, isolation, and disdain.

While parents are giving thought to preparations for their children's Christmas, for example, let me earnestly suggest that you consider giving them the gifts of sensitivity and generosity. Talk to your children and among yourselves about the complex causes of mental illness, emotional distress, and retardation. Let our children know that within that person who seems different, a person whom they might fear or shun, there is an extraordinarily unique person loved by God from all eternity. While encased for the time being in a human habitat that does not function exactly the same way as the rest of us, the sacredness of that individual is crying out to be recognized.

Talk to your children about the importance of going out of their way to be kind to people that others might avoid. Encourage them to invite children who face these problems into their games and other activities. Parents who can do this will give their children a gift of far greater value than any tricycle, bicycle, or other gift that won't last much longer than the Christmas tree. You will be giving them the extraordinary gift of compassion.

Many people with the problems that I'm discussing either stay away or are kept away from parish activities because they know the meaning of rejection. Parishes and parish organizations should go out of their way to identify these people and invite them into our spiritual home.

One of the great messages of Our Lord and Savior Jesus Christ is that he was so at home with those who are different—the despised tax collector, the poor, the prostitute, the lame and the crippled, and the emotionally disturbed. Can we truly claim to be His followers and not attempt to imitate Him in this regard?

MARRIAGE, DIVORCE, AND RE-MARRIAGE

"I love you with my whole heart.
You're the center of my world. We'll be together forever!"
— King Henry VIII to Catherine of Aragon (alleged)

In the developed world, Roman Catholic dioceses have almost universally set up a system of ecclesiastical courts that can handle anything that goes wrong within the Church. These courts are properly set up according to ecclesiastical law, and they are capable of handling any conflicts within the diocese, but in point of fact, the vast majority of its work has to do with marriage. For this reason, these courts are commonly referred to as matrimonial tribunals.

These tribunals are usually located in the diocesan offices. The diocesan bishop appoints the members. Lay people can serve on these tribunals, but only if they have a thorough grounding in ecclesiastical law. There are usually two or three people involved. If a couple has separated and one or both are seeking a declaration of nullity (better known as an annulment), the tribunal will carefully hear the case from both sides. When they are doing this, they are alleging that something was present in the marriage that blocked the sacrament of matrimony. If the tribunal agrees with the petition, there is an automatic appeal to the next higher court. If the tribunal rejects the petition for annulment, then that is the end of the issue. If one party does not like the decision, he or she can appeal to the Roman Rota (the highest court in the Catholic Church).

Why do cases come before these tribunals? First, the Church teaches that a valid Christian marriage binds the couple until death. Secondly, a large percentage of marriages in this country (including among Catholics) fail, ending in divorce, and so the former spouses frequently seek to clarify their marital status inside the life of the Catholic Church.

Every Catholic has a right to approach one of these courts if he or she feels that they want to challenge the validity of their marriage. They may have a right to apply, but securing their goal is not easy.

Let me start by distinguishing the difference between a marriage and a wedding. In general, our society does not concern itself with the distinction between these two words, but in the Catholic Church they are extraordinarily important. Larger society would consider any wedding that takes place with a valid government license and a proper person officiating—from a Justice of the Peace to a ship's captain—as a marriage. We admit that all are weddings, but a much smaller portion of them are true marriages. Marriage is one of seven sacraments given to the Church by Jesus Christ. Marriage creates a sacred bond between the man and the woman, and that bond will be intact until one or the other dies.

However, a *Christian* marriage requires a number of factors to be present to so bind the couple. First, both parties must be baptized. Secondly, both parties must clearly understand what it is that they are doing. Both parties must be entering this relationship freely. Both must intend a permanent union. Both people have to be open to the possibility of children. If any one of these requirements were missing, the Church would consider the event not to be a valid sacrament.

Given the diversity of our culture, the different value systems, and the complex social relationships from which brides and grooms are drawn, it frequently happens that something is lacking which therefore prevents a definitive celebration of the sacrament.

When a person—not always a Catholic (sometimes it's a Protestant married to a Catholic)—wants to challenge the validity of their marriage, they go to the tribunal and file a petition for a declaration of nullity. If one or more of these essential components for matrimony is missing and can be proven, the Church will grant a declaration of nullity, thus allowing that person to marry again within the Catholic Church.

Let's look at the factors individually.

Baptism is the first and most necessary sacrament, and should precede the reception of all other sacraments. Therefore, baptism is necessary on both sides. The Church respects the initial marriage between a couple even if one has not been baptized, but the Church does not consider that marriage a sacrament.

Secondly, both parties must have enough maturity to clearly understand what they are doing. Regretfully, in our society many young men and women marry and lack the maturity that is necessary for entering into the sacrament of matrimony.

The third factor is freedom. Classically, this is violated in a situation where the young lady is pregnant, and she feels coerced by family to get married, but this can occur in other settings as well.

Finally, you must intend a permanent union. If a guy shows up three weeks into a marriage with lipstick on his collar, it is clear that he never intended this to be a permanent union. Telling a friend about these kinds of issues will count as proof for the tribunal. If it can be shown that in a man's mind what was really present was, "I love you with my whole heart— I'd like to marry you for... a year and half," the tribunal will declare that marriage null and void from the beginning.

Finally, you have to be open to the possibility of having children, and this *must be more than simply being on the Pill.* The Pill simply reflects that the couple is trying to avoid conception at that time. There must be a statement of refusal to have kids. Again, as long as another person besides the spouse has heard this statement, that will count for the tribunal.

Don't let all this discussion of nullifying factors confuse you about the Church's solemn commitment to permanent Christian marriage. The Church is absolutely so committed. When a wedding is approaching, the Church does many things to help prepare the couple for this undertaking, to assist the couple in becoming the important formers of a new unit in our society, and a new cell in the life of the Church. This is tremendously important. However, people make mistakes, and if one has been made, the Church will do whatever it can to improve the situation.

SOLVING THE LACK
OF PRIESTLY SUPPLY

"The priesthood and the Eucharist in the Catholic Church cannot be separated, and we cannot bring the Eucharist to people without priests. The present system of utilizing the priesthood has got to be examined."
—*Bishop McCarthy, in an interview in American-Statesman Magazine*

The Church that Jesus Christ established is essentially a missionary entity. It begins with Jesus' command to go forth from Jerusalem and Judea and Samaria, and ultimately to the ends of the earth, to teach the gospel that He has left us. It is to endeavor to reach the population of the entire world. That was 2,000 years ago, and we're running a little behind schedule.

Today, the population of Christians is approaching two billion. Of that number, considerably more than half are in the Roman Catholic Church. The other Christian churches also have a strong Christian thrust, but I'm just talking about the Roman Catholics, and specifically the Catholic Church in the U.S.A.

How is the Church doing in its missionary activities? Well, there are lots of Catholics, but our numbers are not growing very rapidly. An argument can be made that membership is actually shrinking. One of the clichés is that fallen-away Catholics are the largest Christian group in the country—what a tragedy! What is causing this?

There are many reasons for our weak thrust in evangelization; some of them, such as the marriage laws of the Catholic Church, can be addressed in another context. Here I would like to touch on the shortage of native priests—a shortage that is approaching catastrophic proportions—and this shortage is growing more severe year by year.

The ordained priest is the center of the organizational structure of the Church. It's not really the priest himself, but the sacramental reality by which Jesus is present in the local Christian community. The method of bringing Christ's presence into a concrete moment is, of course, the sacramental system. But, this sacramental system without a priestly presence is extraordinarily weak. Let me tell you what I mean by that. People can still witness marriage, you can still have baptisms, but there is no Eucharist, Confirmation, Reconciliation, or Last Rites. *Five of the seven sacraments require ordination.*

How is the Church attempting to respond to this extraordinarily difficult situation? There are a number of possible ways. Resurrecting the diaconate has enabled large parishes once served by many priests to get by with one or two priests while utilizing a half-dozen deacons.

One of the most common modes of operation around the country is that Bishops in the United States are reaching out to developing nations, third-world countries, and drawing in both seminarians and priests to serve in the American parishes. I say "third-world" because the first world, Europe, is having problems equal to this country, and even worse! We're not getting more priests from Ireland. These Bishops would much rather have priests produced by their own local dioceses, but they are in ever shorter supply. Covering all the parishes' sacramental needs is simply not possible. And so, often without much enthusiasm, the American bishops accept priests from Nigeria, Tanzania, Sri Lanka, India, Pakistan, Colombia, and similar places.

If these priests are already ordained at the time of their arrival, they are often put to work immediately in a parish that needs their sacramental powers. It's not stretching the truth to say that many are met at the airport, driven to the parish of their assignment, and handed their letter of appointment. If you are just in from Sri Lanka, you'll have a real shock on Sunday morning!

Speaking for the short term, the Church is blessed to have the services of these foreign priests. They are needed. They want to be here. Most of all, they are validly ordained. Valid ordination is important for the sacramental life of the parish, but *is valid ordination alone adequate to enable a priest from a distant land to be effective not just in a new culture, but in a new culture that is at dramatic variance with what he has ever known?*

Using an inordinate number of foreign priests solves one serious problem, but brings on a multitude of other problems. The first one to manifest in nearly every case is the question of language. English is the international language; so many priests from Pakistan, Uganda, and India arrive speaking English. If the truth were known, however, they arrive speaking *their* brand of English. In many cases, they are very well educated and want to be of real service to the Church in the United States. But, if they cannot be understood on Sunday morning, their presence may be a very limited blessing.

Many dioceses in the United States have endeavored to provide some modest amount of re-orientation for newly arriving foreign priests. Sometimes it's a one-week seminar; sometimes it's a one-week seminar annually for three years, but how does that compare to being born, raised, educated, and ordained for another country?

These seminars don't even begin to solve the problem of cultural adaptation. What is to be done? The answer to that unites all the Bishops in this country. They want to see an increase in vocations among American Catholics. They have tried hard. They have given vocation directors special training. Over the last forty years, vocation offices have been established. Budgets have been expanded. Publications have been developed. Psychological testing and other professional aids have been developed. Sadly, to date, the level of native vocations continues to decline.

We here in the United States are not the only ones battling this issue. I think too, of Brazil, a nation of about two hundred million people. Half a century ago, they were almost 100 percent baptized Catholics. Today, at least one third of them have left the Church. *The primary reason for this painful exodus is a grossly inadequate supply of priests.* In Brazil and other South American countries, most villages literally only get to see a priest ONCE per year! In that brief visit, the priest baptizes all the babies born in the last year, witnesses communal marriage ceremonies, and walks around blessing the graves of the dead. I believe this loss would not have occurred if the Church would have provided adequate priestly services, the Eucharist, and religious formation, but the Church did not and is not doing it now.

Closer to home we note that in 1962, there were approximately 38 million Roman Catholics in the United States served by 55,000 Catholic priests. In 2002, there were 62 million Roman Catholics served by 37,000 priests. Is there a rocket scientist in the house? Is the only option drawing into this wealthy country priests from poor, undeveloped countries that desperately need these vocations themselves? Or, should we be preparing to live with a Church that is almost devoid of a realistic priestly supply?

The answer, of course, is no—*there is another option*. Celibacy was not present in the apostolic church. Celibacy manifested itself only in a very limited way in the first four or five centuries, and it was not made a condition in universal cannon law until the 12th century. I believe that many would admit that it has never been universally successful!

In the present structure of the Church, our Holy Father, the Bishop of Rome, could, if he chose, change this policy with an act of his will and his simple signature at the bottom of a document, thus making celibacy an optional requirement for the western Church. My personal belief is that this change- which would truthfully only be a reversion back to earlier Catholic tradition- would remove a major obstacle to more Americans choosing the priesthood as a vocation, and thus would greatly help to solve the problem of dwindling priestly supply.

THE MISSION OF THE CHURCH

"I'm a frustrated missionary."
—Bishop John McCarthy, remembering his high school days

The Catholic Church is far and away the largest organization on the planet that has members who belong purely by choice. For example, there are more Chinese than there are Roman Catholics, but as a membership organization, the Church is the largest. Our Church has grown slowly over the centuries. Quite frankly, for those of us who are interested in the *innate missionary thrust* of the Church, it's grown all too slowly. ***Our Church has the responsibility of being committed to presenting the salvific message of Jesus Christ- here, there, and everywhere; today, tomorrow and forever!***

Remember this: the essence of the Church is to tell the joyful story of God's love for the whole human family. This love is always being manifested in the good things all around us, but it's most clear in the fact that God Himself—the Infinite Being that we worship—chose to step into the human story and join humanity. That's what Jesus of Nazareth is always all about. We're dealing with a very real human being in whom God dwells. It's a great love story! God is pleased with the totality of creation. The apex of His creation is the free human beings that God brought into existence. These beings have two glorious powers: the power to think and the power to love. One purpose of creation is that human beings come to understand God's love for them and respond to that love.

The mission of the Church is to bring that idea forward, constantly and everywhere. In Uganda, in South Bend, Indiana, in Tokyo, wherever the Church is, to tell us this morning, and Sunday, and next month, and every day that God loves the human family. The reality of God's love should be so overpowering to us that we're not worried about cancer, economics, family conflicts, chaos—all the things that we do worry about. I am not saying that they're not important, but these worries are not nearly as important as the awesome reality that we have been brought into existence by an Infinite Being that loves us. Period.

This is not all that obvious. The average parish is tremendously turned in upon itself. I think that it has always been this way, and probably always will be, because of human nature. We're all somewhat self-centered as individuals and as institutions. If you looked at a parish's income, say an urban parish in central Texas in 2008, their income might be one or two million dollars. I can guarantee you that if they are like the average parish, they would be giving less than one percent to missionary activity. Now, virtually every Catholic church has within it one or two missionaries from such places as Africa or Indonesia, and these wonderful men and women come in and speak at all the Masses on a given Sunday, taking up a collection for their particular missionary organization. The role of the parish is simply to take up that collection and send the money to the Diocesan office for the propagation of the faith (which in turn, coordinates all missionary appeals, thus ensuring that the funds are sent to the proper missionary effort.)

However, I'm talking about all of us getting out of ourselves, out of our regular structure, bringing the knowledge of God and of Jesus to those who do not have it. *So this involves all our brothers and sisters who are Christian reaching out to the large populations here at home, as well as Asia, Africa, and some parts of South America in the interior that don't know the story of God's love for the human family.* The Church is supposed to do that, to put this story forward constantly.

The sad thing is that we do not do that effectively. It's the human condition, as I mentioned earlier. We must struggle against it. I'd like to make a couple of suggestions as to how we could solve this problem, at least in part.

Every parish has an education committee, a liturgy committee, and now (thanks be to God!) a social action committee, to deal with problems within the parish, and all this is well and good. Nevertheless, I think it's also important that every parish have a well-established evangelization committee (also possibly known as a missionary committee). That committee would have as its job the monitoring of all the things that the parish does, and relating them to the spreading of the Gospel. First and foremost, this will involve the development of a strong evangelical consciousness among the parishioners along two layers-both local and global efforts. Yes, that's going to involve bringing in missionaries, motivating some people from the parish to go on missions, and looking for resources to assist them to do that. *But it also involves our neighborhoods, our own backyard.* This committee is going to be a constant reminder to all the people in the parish that this spreading of our faith is not just a nice thing to do a couple Sundays a year, but something that the Church should be doing every day, every week, all year long.

For the last hundred years, we have inadvertently given Catholics the impression that missionary work means leaving the country. Not true! We can do missionary work in the line at the cash register in the grocery store. We can do missionary work when we are visiting our neighbors who happen to be ill. We can do missionary work *wherever we have the opportunity to talk about faith.* Remember this, though- nobody is ever drawn to Jesus Christ by argumentation. It is FAITH that begets faith.

By the way, we're not out to convert a dedicated Methodist. If we're not just talking about Africa and Asia, but the tens of millions of people in the United States who are "unchurched"- many of who are Christians- what do we do about them? A very small percentage of the population will say they are atheist, or that they don't have any church. Personally, I use this question to define a person's religious affiliation: what do they say they are when they check into a hospital? In the United States, the majority will say Catholic, Methodist, Presbyterian, Baptist, or some other Christian denomination. However, the awesome reality of God's love for them is not paramount in their lives, so therefore, they choose not to respond to it. *How do you try to reach these people?* It's not easy.

In our country, we tend to keep our practice of religion slightly out of sight so that we don't offend anybody or step on anybody's toes. In reality, there are dozens of different things to do to bring the message of the Church into a wider view. One that worked well twenty or thirty years ago—and I don't know why we're not still using it—is old-fashioned advertising. The Knights of Columbus ran national ads: do you want to know about Catholicism? Write to this address. You want instructions through the mail? We'll send them to you. And tens of thousands of people responded to that. The Catholic Church is absurdly shy about this venue. If you open the newspaper on Saturday morning and look at church ads, the biggest Catholic Church in town will take out a little two-bit ad, and the others won't bother to advertise at all.

I started a combined ad once where all the Catholic churches went in together the week before Holy Week. We had every one of their schedules there, and it produced tremendous results. I couldn't believe some of the resistance that some of them had. "That's cheap. We don't advertise. That puts us on a level with fundamentalists who are just trying to build a big congregation." Now, you can't be crude about it. But it's important to remember that you're not advertising the Church so much as finding a way to begin to tell the story of Jesus of Nazareth.

A measurable part of the Church's effort and energy should be going towards missionary activity. We have a long way to go. *Let's get busy!*

We have so deep a faith. People listen when you offer to remember their sick or dead loved one in your night prayers. My husbands uncle EM was a Deacon Baptist in a clergy type at his church — One day he and wife aunt Velma said to me, We watch the way you take your little girls to your church each & every Sunday even if you have been very late to get home after being at a Rodeo or Horse Show. Many times my daily life & my childrens leave the peace of our faith with friends & relatives of other Faith. I never give a Sermon, I just live my life as I feel our Lords expects me too & a reassuring 4 children with example of being at Holy Mass during the week & always visiting our Lord when we were near a Catholic Church! He was & is our very lives. Difficult to drive 15 miles to and in alone now

ABOUT BISHOP JOHN MCCARTHY

John Edward McCarthy was born in Houston, Texas, during the early days of the Great Depression. George McCarthy, John's father, worked as a civil engineer, but he died suddenly when John was only eighteen months old. This misfortune left John's mother, Grace, struggling to keep her four young children living together as a family. As if that challenge was not enough, John suffered with serious illness as a young child, culminating in three major abdominal surgeries during his sixth year. Not surprisingly, John subsequently had a rather slow start in team athletics, as the doctors (and John's mother) wisely kept him away from contact sports. At home with primarily adult neighbors to visit with, John began to develop a keen interest in current events and politics. John's mother taught him world geography at the kitchen table, together digesting the daily newspaper articles and mapping out the progression of Hitler's army and potential European counter attacks.

The McCarthy family was largely sustained during the '30's by a generous uncle in New York City who provided monthly stipends of up to $80 whenever possible, but with the coming of World War II costs soared and things were more difficult in the '40's than in the '30's. Although it's true that John never missed a meal, often it was very close. Fortunately, his family received a lot of "free stuff" by way of a wonderful parish priest, Father Matthew Daley, who would come up with turkeys at Thanksgiving and Christmas, and St. Vincent De Paul provided clothing. Of note, John wasn't particularly conscious of being poor. In his words, "Frankly, there wasn't a lot more around to provide a contrast." All three McCarthy boys took part-time jobs, as even a few extra dollars made a big difference. During high

school, John worked in downtown Houston in a petroleum statistics office
running a multi-lift printing press. Since there was still a need for a bit
more money, John also began booking football cards on the side. Perhaps
this is the first evidence of John's future success in fundraising...

Despite being born and raised in Texas, John was and is 100 percent
Irish. Three of John's four grandparents were born in Ireland, and while
his mother, Grace O'Brien, was born in the United States, she grew up in
the very Irish section of lower Manhattan. John's Irish heritage joyfully
permeated his daily life. "My mother sang Irish songs all the time, and she
knew a bit of Gaelic. Being Irish and being Catholic always overlapped- it's
hard to separate them." To this day, John can spontaneously burst forth
in these Irish folksongs from his youth- watch out if your last name is
Harrigan! And John's mother Grace *absolutely believed in St. Patrick's Day.*
John remembers proudly carrying a note to his teacher on March 18th,
stating very clearly: "Dear Sister Mary Margaret, Please excuse John for his
absence from school yesterday. As you know, it was St. Patrick's Day. Many
thanks. Sincerely, Mrs. Grace McCarthy."

Did John always plan on becoming a priest? Not *always.* His high school
classmates remember him as school editor, president of the student council
and president of the senior class, with a very active dating life. However,
in his senior year, John realized he needed to start thinking seriously about
his life plan, and he had, indeed, given a lot of thought to the priesthood.
John saw the priesthood as "a happy life, with unique opportunities to help
others, to support the little guy." He began studies the summer after high
school at St. Mary seminary, and with the passage of each year, steadily
confirmed that the priesthood was his true calling.

John is the product of a life-long Catholic education, beginning with
his first grade in All Saints School in the Houston Heights, through St.
Thomas High School and to graduation from the University of St. Thomas,
majoring in economics and sociology. He received a seminary education
at St. Mary's Seminary and the School of Theology at the University of
St. Thomas. Ordained in 1956, his first assignment was at St. Pius Parish
in Pasadena, an industrial suburban area. Fr. John's second parish was
the well-established St. Cecilia's in an affluent section of Houston. With

his third assignment, Fr. John became the pastor at his home parish, the "delightfully Polish and Czech-infused" All Saints Parish.

In 1966, Fr. John began one of his three assignments outside of the Diocese of Galveston-Houston. He started in San Antonio, placed in an office focusing on migrant workers as part of the Bishops' Committee for the Spanish Speaking. Then, Fr. John moved up to the national level, relocating to the U.S. Catholic Conference Social Action Department in Washington D.C. for a couple years. When he was able to return to Houston as the pastor of St. Theresa's, John began to develop his views and ideas for getting parishes more deeply involved with the immediate neighborhoods in which they were functioning, thus creating the first organized parish social ministries.

Fr. John was concerned by the fact that while every parish without exception had organized programs on worship and education, they did not necessarily have anything structured to address their local social needs. Fr. John has always believed that the nature of the parish is to "make Jesus present at this particular place, in this particular time." Fr. John likes to break down the work of Jesus into three categories- worship, teaching and the lessening of pain- and he feels strongly that all three of these activities should be made real and concrete in every single parish. Therefore, Fr. John considered a parish to be incomplete if it did not have a defined, structured and funded social component. John carried this belief forward throughout his ministry, aiming to see a program for social concerns established at every single parish.

While working in parish life, John renewed a close friendship with his former high school classmate, Father Bill Woods, a Maryknoll Missioner. Their vocational journeys together reached isolated communities within the jungles of Guatemala, and sparked in John a strong interest in helping missions overseas. This commitment was further strengthened after Father Woods was tragically assassinated, one of many martyrs in Central America during that time.

The Bishops of Texas asked for John to be released from his local parish duties to lead the Texas Catholic Conference (TCC). John's role was to coordinate (whenever possible) the varied activities being carried out by the eleven dioceses that existed within Texas at that time. Today, Texas has grown to fifteen dioceses, making the TCC the largest state conference in the nation. John really loved that job, finding it especially "wonderful to be working on an issue in El Paso on one day and be in Beaumont the next." (Emphasizing that although these two communities officially reside in the same state, they have dramatically different cultures, economies, attitudes and issues.) He was involved in every aspect of diocesan activities- from Catholic Charities, to education, to retreat houses, family life services, faith formation, vocations, and seminaries, to name a few.

After seven years leading the TCC, John was appointed by Pope John Paul II to be the Auxiliary Bishop of the Diocese of Galveston-Houston, where he spent the next seven years. John's special interests were in the world of ecumenism, communications and the development of social ministry in the approximately one hundred and fifty parishes in the diocese.

In December of 1985, the Pope John Paul II made John the Bishop of Austin. . While he was in that position, both Central Texas and the Austin Diocese enjoyed substantial growth. Roughly twenty new parishes were created, bringing the total to around one hundred twenty five parishes in the diocese. While working in Austin for fifteen years, Bishop John remained very active in the National Bishops' Catholic Conference, but his principal interest was relief services in the "Third World" which the Conference conducted through Catholic Relief Services, the largest international volunteer program in the world. Since his retirement as the Bishop, John has been "very happy to leave the administrative details of running a diocese to very capable hands of Bishop Joe Vasquez." Bishop John continued, however, to maintain a consistently overflowing calendar-leading retreats, hosting charity events, offering lectures, celebrating masses and writing his blog.

SAINT LOUISE HOUSE

"When you walk into a shelter you are broken. My life and my heart were broken into a million pieces. Saint Louise House has helped me put those pieces back together. When my son and I moved in, and I realized the door that had just closed behind me actually locked, I breathed freely for the first time in almost a year. I knew that I had finally found a home.

Thanks to Saint Louise House, I know that when the time comes for me to move on, I can do so with confidence and self-respect. Saint Louise House offers women in my position a chance to become the women they were always meant to be, and gives their children a chance to thrive in a safe, loving environment."
— **Saint Louise House alumna**

Bishop McCarthy's passion for the rippling impact that Saint Louise House generates in our community is immeasurable. In his words, *"Saint Louise House is quite simply the most meaningful social effort with which I have ever been involved."* This innovative program was created within the Bishop's diocese in the year 2000, led by the Daughters of Charity and parishioners of St. Austin Catholic Church. These dedicated founders answered the call to address the drastic shortage of safe housing and supportive services for homeless women and children.

On the surface, Saint Louise House offers an apartment-style supportive housing program. New families move in to a fully outfitted apartment—with everything from furniture and linens to pots and pans—and when they are ready to move forward, every item goes with them for their next home. Reaching far beyond basic housing, however, Saint Louise

House includes the whole package of case management, counseling, life skills training, and employment services, as well as access to healthcare, education, and child care. Licensed social workers and case managers work with residents to set goals specific to each family, and provide on-site support as they work to become self-sufficient.

Recognizing the dignity and worth of every person, Saint Louise House empowers women to transform their lives, their families, and their community. Any and all profits from the sale of *Off the Cuff & Over the Collar: Common Sense Catholicism* will go to Saint Louise House to help them continue their extraordinary mission.

ACKNOWLEDGEMENTS

This collective project has a number of distinct beginnings that I'd like to recognize. Tom Borders was interested in having me review on videotape a wide range of pastoral issues with which the Church is currently dealing. Drs. Drew and Jill Grimes frequently heard my homilies to young students, and felt my basic explanations of Catholic traditions (as well as my ideas on teasing, bullying, gossiping, fear, and other universal topics) merited greater distribution. I'm especially thankful to Tom, Drew and Jill, because without them, *Off the Cuff & Over the Collar: Common Sense Catholicism* would never have fully materialized.

I offer special thanks to Katherine Mayfield, our external developmental editor, for her objective perspective and edits. Thanks to Lynn Lampert for her photography. I'd like to recognize Kay Mooney, as well as Letty Landa and Mary Bell, for their enthusiasm and efforts to help launch the book. Blessings and thanks to the rest of the team that helped me to create and maintain an online presence, especially Luke Borders, Shelby Stephens, Linda Miller, and Brittany and Nicole Grimes. Finally, I'd like to personally thank Sharon Bieser and her team at Saint Louise House, as well as all the generous men and women who donated to her wonderful organization on behalf of this work.

May God bless each of you with extraordinary passion, ability, and energy to continue doing His will!

SUBJECT INDEX

Again, we are delighted that any and all profits from the sale of *Off the Cuff & Over the Collar: Common Sense Catholicism* will go to Saint Louise House to help them continue their extraordinary mission. Anyone wishing to contribute further in any capacity to this marvelous charity is encouraged to visit their website (http://www.saintlouisehouse.org) for more information, or reach them at their mailing address (Saint Louise House, 2026 Guadalupe Street, Austin, Texas, 78705.)

May the road rise up to meet you.
May the wind always be at your back.
May the sun shine warm upon your face,
and rains fall soft upon your fields.
And until we meet again,
May God hold you in the palm of His hand.

Made in the USA
Lexington, KY
05 March 2014